25 DAYS TO BETTER MACHINE QUILTING

Hands-On Learning to Improve Your Skills

LORI KENNEDY

Martingale®
Create with Confidence

25 Days to Better Machine Quilting:
Hands-On Learning to Improve Your Skills
© 2020 by Lori Kennedy

Martingale®
19021 120th Ave. NE, Ste. 102
Bothell, WA 98011-9511 USA
ShopMartingale.com

Printed in Hong Kong
25 24 23 22 21 20   8 7 6 5 4 3 2 1

Library of Congress Cataloging-in-Publication Data is available upon request.

ISBN: 978-1-68356-077-7

MISSION STATEMENT

We empower makers who use fabric and yarn to make life more enjoyable.

CREDITS

PUBLISHER AND CHIEF VISIONARY OFFICER
Jennifer Erbe Keltner

CONTENT DIRECTOR
Karen Costello Soltys

DESIGN MANAGER
Adrienne Smitke

MANAGING EDITOR
Tina Cook

PRODUCTION MANAGER
Regina Girard

ACQUISITIONS AND DEVELOPMENT EDITOR
Laurie Baker

PHOTOGRAPHERS
Adam Albright
Brent Kane

TECHNICAL EDITOR
Nancy Mahoney

ILLUSTRATOR
Sandy Loi

COPY EDITOR
Sheila Chapman Ryan

DEDICATION

Dedicated to my mother, Dorothy Crawley, who always did small things with great love

Contents

INTRODUCTION

Free-motion quilting should be fun! It's the final step in turning our patchwork and appliqué into cherished quilts and heirlooms. When you do your own quilting, you can choose whimsical motifs or dramatic patterns, and you can add doodled illustrations and leave hidden messages. You can use thread to create fabulous focus motifs, elegant textures, and glowing special effects. When you have fun quilting, your quilts are fun!

Unfortunately, free-motion quilting strikes fear in the hearts of too many quilters. They let quilt tops languish on shelves while they start cutting and piecing the next quilt top. After spending hours piecing and appliquéing, some quilters are afraid of ruining their beautiful quilt tops with quilting!

Never fear! Machine quilting is just a series of steps, a few techniques, and a little knowledge. It's easier to learn than driving a car. You passed your driver's test, right? Well, even if you didn't, you can still learn to machine quilt in 25 days!

This book is for all skill levels, from novice to advanced, and this book is for YOU if:

+ You're afraid of machine quilting or don't know where to start.

+ You want to have confidence that your quilt won't be ruined by your quilting.

+ You're eager to learn techniques to make the process easier and more creative.

+ You want to try new threads, motifs, and tools.

+ You want to add personal touches to your quilts.

+ You want to create quilts that reflect your personal style.

Each lesson in this book is an in-depth review of a technique or material and includes a project to demonstrate the key points. Most lessons will take less than an afternoon. The samples are small so you can learn the technique quickly, but the techniques are applicable to large projects too. Most skills can be applied right away to a quilt top in your collection.

Each lesson builds on a previous lesson to introduce new techniques and materials while creating more complex quilt designs, so it's best to follow them in order. The goal is to sample as many techniques, supplies, and materials as possible so you can find the products and work flow that works best for you.

Some of the lessons will result in small quilts that can be bound and used as table toppers or wall hangings. Others are intended as a simple way to learn a technique or test a material. Use the instructions as a starting point for your own designs. Make the samples larger or smaller and consider using patchwork blocks in place of wholecloth quilts. Choose your favorite colors to create samples that reflect your personal style. Audition a wide variety of motifs from *Free-Motion Machine Quilting 1-2-3* and *More Free-Motion Machine Quilting 1-2-3* (Martingale, 2017 and 2018, respectively) to create your own designs.

Many of the lessons are great to work on with a friend, small quilt group, or a large guild. Share thread, batting, marking tools, and your own tricks as you work through the lessons. See how many variations your group can create by using different colors, threads, motifs, and batting. Be sure to share your work online at #lorikennedyquilts and #martingaletpp.

By the time you've completed the lessons, whether it takes you 25 days, 25 weeks, or longer, you'll feel confident about choosing the right materials and the best techniques for every project—and you'll have the skills to finish quilts that reflect your personal style.

I hope you're excited to get started!

~Lori

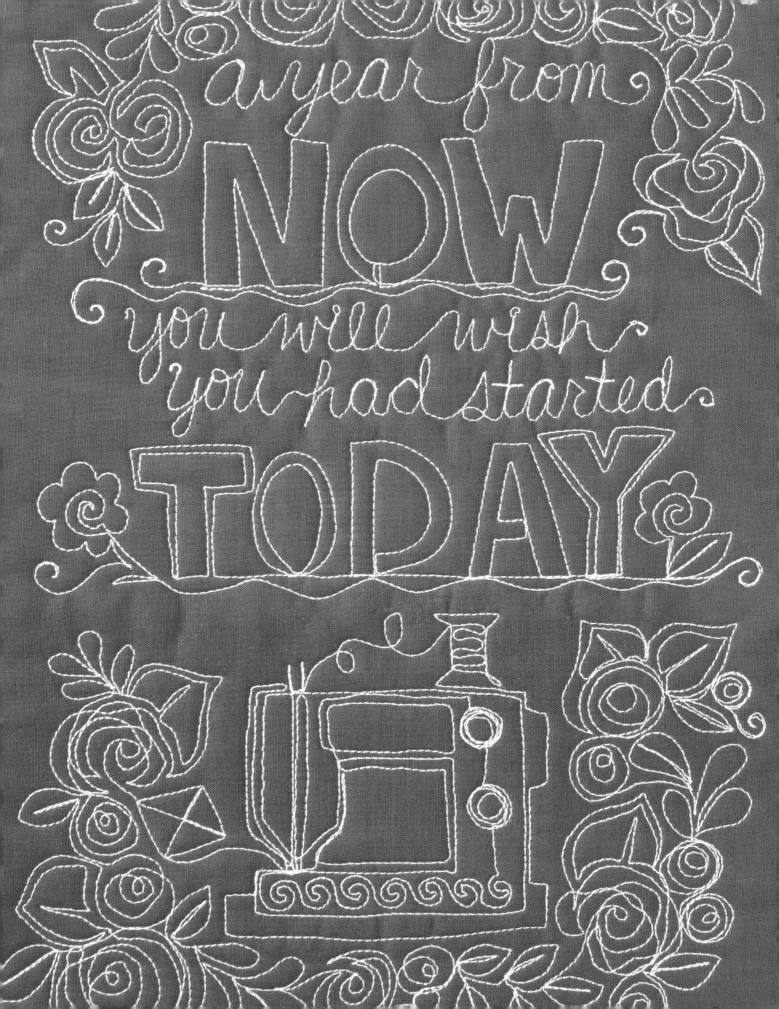

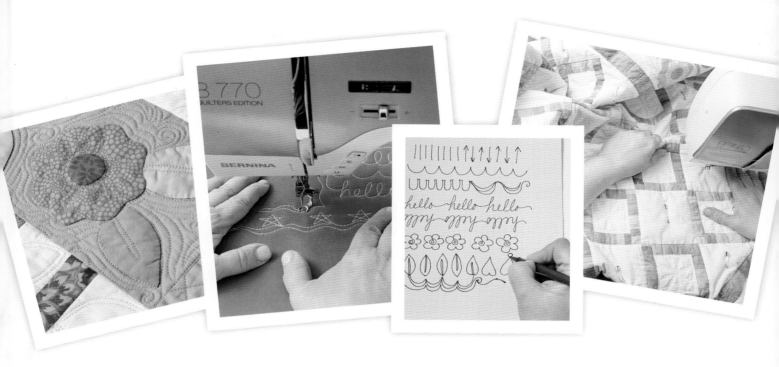

LESSON OVERVIEW

Each lesson is an in-depth review of a machine-quilting technique, supply, or material that builds on previous lessons. It's best to complete the lessons in order. Most lessons include instructions for using the material or practicing the skill on a small sample. The structure of the practice includes a typical workflow for creating a new quilt and ends with a brief evaluation. The following steps and materials apply to each practice session, unless otherwise noted in the instructions.

1. Doodle on paper.

2. Create or select a premade quilt sandwich, then mark it as needed.

3. Choose thread.

4. Set up the machine for free-motion stitching.

5. Stitch.

6. Evaluate.

Make sure your sewing machine is in good working order, and keep the sewing-machine manual handy. To set up your machine for free-motion quilting, disengage the feed dogs and use a free-motion quilting or embroidery foot (see page 8 for more details).

Stitch the outlines and motifs on the quilt following the instructions, or choose your favorite motifs to personalize your project. Complete every project with your machine-quilted signature and date. That way, at the end of 25 days, you can compare your stitching and see how you've improved.

Evaluating your work is an important part of the learning process. After completing every lesson, review your work. Don't be overly critical, but rather use the review as an opportunity to understand the materials and processes. Consider carefully what worked and what didn't, and try to determine why.

12-Step Setup for Free-Motion Quilting

Most of the following steps will be explained in greater detail in the indicated lesson.

1. Clean and oil your machine (fig. A). For any machinery, regular cleaning and oiling helps protect against early wear and tear. For sewing machines, regular maintenance is imperative to creating well-formed stitches. The needle passes through the throat plate and the bobbin rotates hundreds of times per minute with precision timing. Lint buildup from the batting and lack of oil can throw off the timing and cause tension problems as well as skipped or broken stitches.

2. Thread the bobbin (fig. B). See lesson 12, page 58, for details.

3. Attach a single-hole throat plate. The throat plate is the metal piece that sits below the needle and covers the bobbin mechanism. It has slots to accommodate the feed dogs and a hole where the needle passes through and into the bobbin area. Most throat plates have a wide hole to accommodate zigzag and other decorative stitches (fig. C, bottom). While machine quilting, a single-hole throat plate (fig. C, top) helps support the quilt from underneath and prevents it from distorting while the needle pierces the quilt from above. Though not absolutely necessary, a single-hole throat plate helps create the perfect stitch.

4. Attach a table extension (fig. D). See lesson 9, page 44, for details.

5. Position a Supreme Slider (fig. E). This is optional; see lesson 9.

6. Insert a new Topstitch needle (fig. F). Good-quality machine needles are necessary to create a perfect stitch. A tiny burr or bend in a needle can damage thread, fabric, or even the sewing machine. The needle passes through the bobbin and thread flosses through the eye of the bobbin hundreds of times per minute, creating a lot of wear and tear on a small piece of metal! Broken thread and skipped stitches are a sign it's time to change the machine needle.

7. Attach a free-motion quilting foot (fig. G). See lesson 2, page 16.

8. Disengage the feed dogs (fig. H). See lesson 2.

9. Activate the needle-down function (fig. I). See lesson 5, page 26.

10. Thread the machine (fig. J). See lesson 12, page 58.

11. Stitch a test sample and adjust tension as needed (fig. K). See lesson 6, page 30.

12. Begin stitching (fig. L).

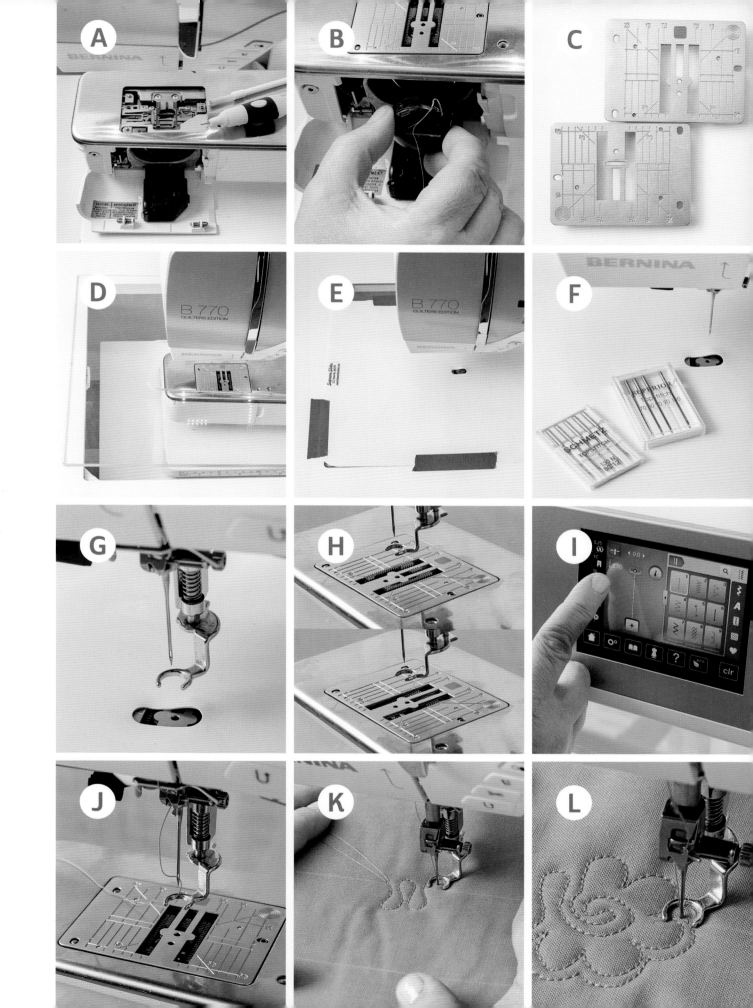

SUPPLIES AND TOOLS

The following list of supplies includes specific tools and materials I frequently use and recommend. It's intended as reference as you work through the lessons, not a list of supplies required to begin quilting. I suggest that you start with the thread and batting you have on hand and try new materials to create different design goals as you learn new techniques. Likewise add tools, stencils, and other supplies to make quilting easier as you try new skills.

Be sure to check the supplies listed for each lesson before you begin. If you can't find the supplies needed at your local quilt shop, you can search for them online.

BOOKS

For additional motif ideas to use in the lessons, you may also like the following books (fig. A).

+ *Free-Motion Machine Quilting 1-2-3*
+ *More Free-Motion Machine Quilting 1-2-3*
+ *180 Doodle Quilting Designs* (Martingale, 2016)
+ *180 More Doodle Quilting Designs* (Martingale, 2018)

THREAD

All you need to know about thread (fig. B) is covered in lesson 12, page 58. At right are lists of heavyweight, mediumweight, and lightweight threads you might like to try.

HEAVYWEIGHT

+ 28-weight cotton by Aurifil
+ 30-weight cotton by Sulky
+ 40-weight King Tut cotton by Superior
+ 40-weight Magnifico polyester by Superior
+ 40-weight rayon by Sulky
+ 30-weight Mirage rayon by Wonderfil
+ 35-weight Twister Tweed rayon by Robison-Anton

MEDIUMWEIGHT

+ 50-weight cotton by Aurifil
+ 50-weight Cotton + Steel cotton by Sulky
+ 50-weight So Fine! polyester by Superior

LIGHTWEIGHT

+ 80-weight cotton by Aurifil
+ 60-weight PolyLite polyester by Sulky
+ 60-weight Bottom Line polyester by Superior
+ 100-weight MicroQuilter polyester by Superior

TOPSTITCH NEEDLES

Topstitch needles (fig. C) have a large eye and a deep, long groove to protect the thread as it moves through the fabric and batting layers. Choose the needle size based on the thread weight you're using. Start with a 90/14 needle. If you notice poor stitch formation or broken stitches, change to a different size needle. Keep topstitch needles in a variety of sizes handy at all times.

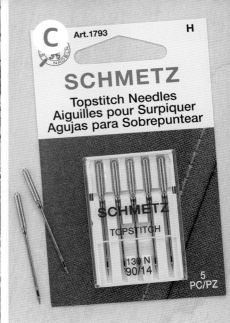

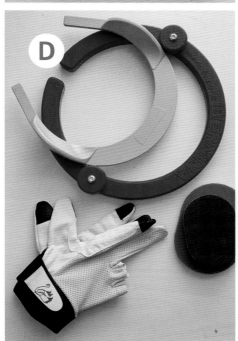

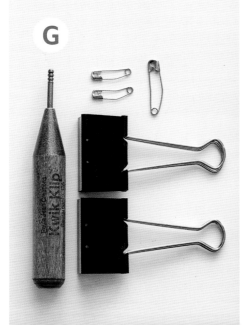

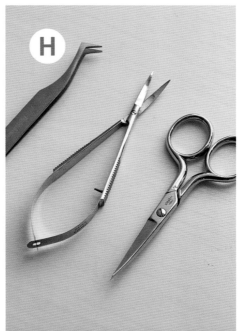

BATTING

Batting comes in a variety of fiber contents, lofts (thicknesses), and sizes. You can learn more about batting in lesson 13, page 66. Here you'll find a listing of various types of batting by fiber content that I like to use.

COTTON

- Warm and Natural low-loft cotton batting by The Warm Company
- Warm and Plush medium-loft cotton batting by The Warm Company
- Quilters Dream cotton (available in four lofts from low to medium loft)

POLYESTER

- Tuscany Polyester by Hobbs
- Soft and Bright by The Warm Company

COTTON/POLYESTER BLEND

- Heirloom Premium 80/20 by Hobbs
- 80/20 Warm by The Warm Company
- 70/30 Quilters Dream Blend for Machines

WOOL

- Tuscany Wool by Hobbs
- Quilter's Dream Wool

WOOL/COTTON BLEND

- Tuscany Wool/Cotton Blend by Hobbs

QUILTING SUPPLIES

- Quilting Gloves (fig. D, page 11).
- Grip & Stitch Quilting Discs by Clever Craft Tools (fig. D).
- Supreme Slider (lesson 9, page 44).
- Sewer's Aid Thread Lubricant (lesson 22, page 108).
- Sew Steady Table (lesson 9, page 44).

Gripping the Quilt

All of the products listed below are designed to help improve your grip while stitching.

Quilting gloves. *Coated fingertips help grip the quilt sandwich and allow better control of the quilt and the quilting line. Many types are available, including brands that leave the index fingers and thumbs free for threading and knotting.*

Quilting hoops. *These sit on top of the quilt layers and help grip and move the quilt while free-motion quilting. Hoops come in a variety of sizes and weights; choose one that feels comfortable to your hands and that fits your work surface.*

Quilting discs. *Quilting discs, like Grip & Stitch by Clever Craft Tools, are soft pads that help grip the quilt without the need for gloves. The discs can be held in one or both hands and are helpful when stitching the edge of a quilt where a hoop can not fit.*

Other gripping options. *Any product that reduces slip on your fingers is worth trying. Nonslip shelf liners, rubber gloves, and some hand lotions can give you better control while quilting.*

MARKING TOOLS

You'll learn more about marking quilt tops in lesson 14, page 72, but these are some of the marking tools I like to use (fig. E, page 11).

+ Dritz chalk cartridge
+ Clover Chaco Liner
+ Crayola Ultra-Clean markers
+ Air-erasable markers

White Chalk

White chalk is easy to see and easy to erase, making it one of the best all-around marking tools for medium to dark fabrics. Use chalk to mark major quilting lines and keep it by your sewing machine so that you can add small spacing marks while working. After quilting, remove the chalk by brushing lightly with a microfiber cloth or by washing the quilt.

STENCILS

Marking grids and other designs is easier with stencils (fig. F, page 11). You can learn more in lesson 17, page 84.

+ Line Design 10" × 10" (SCL-457-10) by The Stencil Company
+ Square Grid 12" (1" Design) (SCL-455-12) by The Stencil Company

BASTING SUPPLIES

Carefully layering the quilt top, batting, and backing is an important part of the quilting process. A few tools can make it easier (fig. G, page 11). Learn more in lesson 18, page 90.

+ 505 Spray and Fix temporary fabric adhesive
+ Kwik clips
+ Safety pins

SCISSORS, SNIPS, AND TWEEZERS

Sewing-machine or bent-tip tweezers are handy for grabbing short bobbin threads and for tying knots. I prefer snips over scissors for cutting threads. Always have a pair ready when free-motion quilting (fig. H, page 11).

DOODLING SUPPLIES

Keep a pen and paper next to your sewing machine to practice your doodles before quilting (fig. I, page 11). Stash notebooks and pens anywhere you are likely to have a few spare minutes away from your sewing machine. (For more about doodling supplies, see lesson 3 on page 19.)

SEWING-MACHINE MANUAL

Keep your sewing-machine manual nearby for reference. If you no longer have one, most are available online. Add bookmarks to the following pages:

+ Cleaning and oiling
+ Tension adjustments
+ Lowering the feed dogs
+ Needle down

LESSON 1:
ORGANIZING FOR QUICK QUILTING

For each lesson, you'll need something to quilt. A quick quilt sandwich is used in many of the lessons and is easy to assemble. You're more likely to spend a few minutes practicing if you have a quilt sandwich handy, so prepare a dozen or so ahead of time to use in the lessons. You'll be ready when inspiration strikes!

WHAT WORKS BEST

A quick quilt sandwich is made of a solid fabric layered with lightweight cotton batting and a suitable backing fabric. A fat quarter measures 18" × 21" and has ample space to quilt and for you to grip the quilt. Smaller pieces don't allow enough room for good hand position.

To see the stitching line best, use a solid fabric on top. For the backing fabric, avoid fabrics that are white-on-white or have a painted or textured surface. These fabrics are slightly more difficult for the needle to penetrate and don't slide as well on the machine work surface. Also avoid fabric that is tightly woven, such as batiks and hand-dyed fabrics. The tight weave is harder for the needle to penetrate and may impact the look of the stitches. Printed fabrics conceal the quilting line while solid fabrics reveal it.

The texture of cotton batting helps it stick to fabrics without adding pins or basting spray. You can use this to your advantage to make quick quilt sandwiches.

WHAT YOU'LL NEED

Makes one quilt sandwich (fig. A).

+ 1 fat quarter of solid fabric for top
+ 1 fat quarter of coordinating print for backing
+ 18" × 21" piece of cotton batting
+ Spray starch

QUICK QUILT-SANDWICH ASSEMBLY

1. Layer the backing (right side down), cotton batting, and the top fabric (right side up) (fig. B).

2. Apply spray starch to the backing fabric to help the quilt sandwich slide more easily while free-motion quilting (fig. C).

3. Press the three layers from the back first and then again from the top (fig. D).

LESSON 2:

LET'S GET STARTED!

Free-motion machine quilting doesn't require a special sewing machine or many special tools. Just lower the feed dogs, attach a free-motion presser foot, thread your machine, and go!

WHAT YOU'LL NEED

+ 1 quick quilt sandwich (page 14)
+ Free-motion quilting foot or embroidery foot
+ Top thread in a color that will show well on your fabric
+ Bobbin thread in a color of your choice
+ Tweezers
+ Snips
+ Quilting gloves (optional)

READY, SET, GO

Let's start by making a quilted record of your current skill level. In this exercise, you'll thread the sewing machine, lower the feed dogs, attach a quilting foot, and stitch. That's really all you need to free-motion quilt any quilt top! Use any fabric and batting you have on hand. Sign and date your work, free-motion style, of course. At the end of the 25 days, you'll be able to see your progress.

1. Disengage the feed dogs, referring to your sewing-machine manual as needed. The feed dogs are the metal bars with teeth located just beneath the throat plate. In regular sewing, the feed dogs advance the fabric through the sewing machine. While free-motion quilting, *you* want to control how fast and in what direction the fabric moves; therefore, you need to disengage the feed dogs. On most machines, you can lower the feed dogs with the touch of a button or lever. On some older machines, you'll need to cover the feed dogs with a plate that came with the machine. (See the photos on page 9 for lowering the feed dogs.)

2. Set up your machine for quilting by inserting a new needle and threading the top and bobbin.

3. Attach a free-motion quilting foot. Several styles of free-motion quilting and embroidery feet are available. Choose a foot that gives you the greatest sewing-area visibility. If available for your sewing machine, look for an offset open-toe foot. (The shank of the foot is set to one side so you can easily see where you are stitching when moving the quilt away from you.) The free-motion embroidery foot #24 from Bernina is my favorite (fig. A).

4. Place the quilt under the needle. With your left hand, hold the top thread taut under the presser foot (fig. B).

5. While still holding the top thread taut, use your right hand to lower the presser foot. Lower the needle with the handwheel or by using a needle-down button if your machine has that feature (fig. C).

6. Raise the needle with the handwheel or needle-up button. With your left hand, quickly tug the top thread, and the loop of bobbin thread should pop to the surface (fig. D).

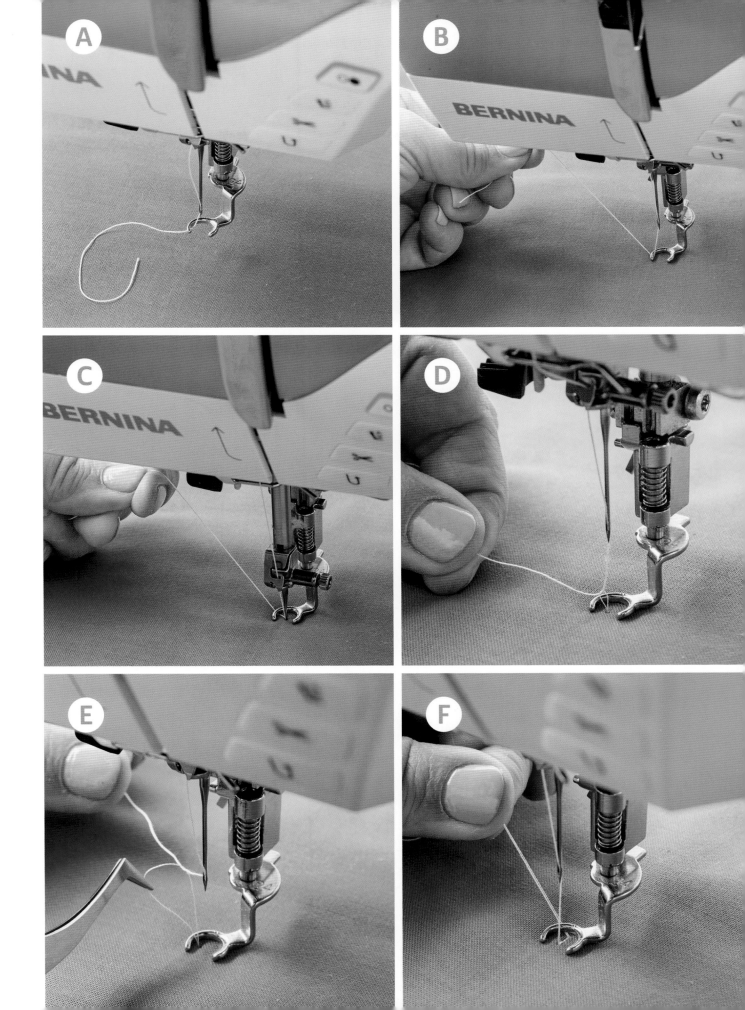

7. Use tweezers to grab the bobbin thread and pull the entire tail of bobbin thread to the top of the quilt to prevent thread from jamming the sewing machine (fig. E, page 17).

Safety First!

The bobbin thread may be very short. For safety, use tweezers to reach under the needle. You never want your hand directly under the needle!

8. Holding both the bobbin and top threads taut, begin stitching by making several very small stitches in place to create a simple beginning knot (fig. F, page 17). Trim the thread tails as soon as it's convenient to pause stitching.

STITCH

Stitch for at least 20 minutes. Fill the quilt sandwich, avoiding the edges of the quilt, where it's difficult to hold the quilt with both hands. Don't spend too much time thinking or planning. Try stitching loops and scallops. Quilt doodles. Write words. Stitch straight or looped lines to travel to different areas within the sample (fig. G). Relax and have fun! End by signing and dating your work.

EVALUATE

Congratulations, you are on your way! Was it easier than you thought? Free-motion quilting is fun and freeing!

18

LESSON 3:
START A DOODLE HABIT

Doodling is the fastest way to improve your machine-quilting skill. Doodling not only allows you to audition motifs for your next quilt, but it improves your eye for spacing, and develops muscle memory. Before quilting each day, spend five minutes doodling on paper as a warm-up to free-motion quilting. Whether you're a born doodler or you've never doodled, it's time to start a quilt-doodle habit!

WHY DOODLE?

Doodling is an important step in learning to free-motion quilt.

Doodling for muscle memory. Every time you draw a motif, you develop muscle memory for the design. This muscle memory allows you to stitch without hesitation and therefore improves the quality of your stitches. Memorizing the movements of creating a motif can save you hours of time by reducing the time spent marking a motif and removing the marking.

Learning a new motif. When you're doodling to practice a motif, copy the motif repeatedly over several sessions until you can draw it without thinking (fig. A, page 21). It may take hundreds of repetitions over several days to create a smooth line. Practice in short sessions while watching TV or talking on the phone. Doodle the motif in a variety of sizes and work out how to travel from one motif to next. When learning a background fill motif, challenge yourself to fill a sheet of paper without lifting the pencil or crossing over any other line. Doodle new motifs repeatedly on scrap paper so you can throw it away or use a method that can be erased easily. If you create a doodle you want to save, cut it out and tape it into a sketchbook, or take a photo with your phone for future reference.

Doodling to evaluate a quilt design.
Doodling is also an important step in the design process. Doodling helps you determine the best motifs for the style and theme of your quilt and allows you to create combinations of motifs to fill the shapes of the blocks and borders in your quilt. When you're doodling to evaluate designs, use a more permanent method, such as drawing in a quilt sketchbook, or using a computer-based drawing tool that allows you to save the design. Begin by listing all the shapes and sizes of the blocks in your quilt. Draw the shapes in your sketchbook and begin auditioning motifs (fig. B, page 21).

Once you narrow your motif selections, see how they look on your quilt by doodling on a vinyl overlay, a Boogie Board (see page 20), or with a computer-based program. Consider the traveling lines (stitching between motifs and blocks) that can minimize the number of times knotting off is required.

Doodling to let your mind wander. Doodling aimlessly is an important creative technique that improves machine quilting. Aimless doodling allows you to develop line combinations and motifs (fig. C, page 21). Frequent doodling stimulates creativity, enhances your ability to create smooth lines, and improves your motif spacing. Quilt your doodles as soon as possible to test them as quilt designs.

DOODLING SUPPLIES

Nothing beats doodling with pen and paper! Try a variety of pens, pencils, and markers as well as different types of paper to find your favorite combinations. Or use whatever is closest, from the newspaper to envelopes. If you create a doodle you really like, tape it into a sketchbook.

MY FAVORITES PENS AND PENCILS

Different strokes for different folks—these are my go-to choices (fig. D).

+ **Stabilo All pencils.** I like the texture of these pencils. They write well on every surface.

+ **FriXion pens.** While some quilters like these pens to mark fabric, I prefer to use them for doodling. I love being able to erase.

+ **Tombow brush pens.** The dark ink and the sturdy feel of Tombow brush pens make every doodle look more artistic!

+ **Dixon Ticonderoga pencils 2B.** I've been using these since second grade and still appreciate the look and feel of a good pencil.

+ **Mechanical pencils.** Nothing beats a pencil that's always sharp!

+ **Flair markers.** A great all-purpose marker.

+ **Fountain pens.** The weight and feel of the nib and how the ink creates a dark line make fountain pens great for doodling.

+ **White gel pens.** White gel pens create an opaque line that looks great on dark paper.

SKETCHBOOKS

Use sketchbooks and your favorite pen or pencil to keep all of your doodles in one place for ready reference when you sit down to stitch. Try new motifs and combinations. Rehearse ways to fill the shapes within your quilt. Add inspirational photos and ideas for templates. Keep several sketchbooks wherever you doodle, including lined, graph, and grid paper in a variety of sizes.

In addition to pads designed for writing and drawing, consider doodling on newspaper, repurposed old books, and nontraditional materials. Decide whether you prefer spiral or traditional binding (fig. E).

DRY-ERASE BOARDS

Dry-erase boards are best when you don't plan to save your doodles. Hang a dry-erase board in your sewing space and use markers to repetitively practice new motifs to create muscle memory. Explore motif combinations and try doodling large and small versions of every motif. If you decide to save your doodle, take a photo to store on your phone.

Wet-Erase vs. Dry-Erase Markers

Wet-erase markers require a wet cloth to remove the markings while dry-erase markers are easy to remove with a dry, soft cloth. When doodling on a whiteboard, dry-erase markers are fine; however, I prefer wet-erase markers when testing motifs on vinyl overlay, to prevent smudging the ink onto the fabric.

BOOGIE BOARD WRITING TABLET

Blackboard by Boogie Board is a liquid crystal writing table that's simple to use and doesn't require a computer. It's a great way to practice and audition designs without paper. The design disappears with the push of a button. Lay the board over a quilt block to audition a design or doodle on it to practice a new motif (fig. F). No markers necessary!

COMPUTER APPLICATIONS

Another way to doodle without paper is to use an app for a computer or tablet that allows you to import a photo of a block or quilt and overlay a drawing. Procreate for iOS (iPads) is one I highly recommend.

PRACTICE MAKES (ALMOST) PERFECT

In this practice session, we'll create ways to make doodling easier. Start by collecting doodle supplies, then we'll make a vinyl overlay so you can doodle over quilt tops and test scale in later lessons.

COLLECT YOUR SUPPLIES

Scour your house or make a shopping list. Gather a variety of pens, pencils, and markers. Collect notebooks, paper, and sketchbooks in various sizes and styles so that over time, you can try different combinations of writing papers and marking tools to see what you like best. Place your tools wherever you might doodle: in your purse, car, next to the TV, in the kitchen. The key is to have a pen and paper handy to take advantage of free moments.

DOODLE!

Doodle for at least five minutes, starting with lines, loops, circles, and scallops. Add your name and words. Make marks and see if you can turn them into designs. Try to connect the designs to create continuous-line designs for stitching (fig. G).

MAKE A VINYL OVERLAY

A sheet of lightweight vinyl is a convenient way to test motif ideas. You can lay the vinyl over a quilt and use a wet-erase marker to audition a motif. Use this to check the scale of a motif, plan the stitching order, and work out paths for traveling to other areas within a quilt.

WHAT YOU'LL NEED

+ 20" × 20" square of 12-gauge vinyl (available at many craft stores)
+ 4 strips, 1" × 20", of fabric for binding (or use leftover quilt binding or masking tape)

WRAP THE EDGES

To prevent accidentally drawing off the edge of the vinyl and onto your quilt top, wrap the edges of the vinyl square with fabric, masking tape, or painter's tape for visibility (fig. H).

1. Thread the machine.

2. Set up the machine for zigzag sewing.

3. Press each fabric strip in half, wrong sides together.

4. On each side of the vinyl square, wrap a folded fabric strip over the edge, making sure the vinyl is between the two fabric layers. Zigzag over the edges. Or, wrap the edges with masking tape.

EVALUATE

+ Are you a natural-born doodler or will doodling require more concentration for you?

+ Where in your house are you most likely to doodle?

+ What are your favorite pens/pencils?

+ Do you have a favorite pad of paper?

LESSON 4:

DOODLING AND STITCHING HORIZONTAL MOTIFS

It's best to get your ideas on fabric as soon as inspiration strikes. Keep your machine-quilting supplies handy and a step-by-step setup guide near your machine for reference, and you can be quilting in less than five minutes!

DOODLE FIRST

On lined paper, doodle loops and scallops. Try upside down motifs, as well as small and large motifs. Practice doodling your signature and other words. Doodle from left to right and right to left, since you'll be quilting in both directions.

SUPPLIES

+ 1 quick quilt sandwich (page 14)
+ Top thread (heavyweight thread that contrasts well with the top fabric)
+ Bobbin thread (50-weight or lighter in a color that matches the top thread)

GET READY

1. Use white chalk and a ruler to mark horizontal lines, 1" apart, on the top fabric of the quilt sandwich (fig. A) .
2. Set up your machine for quilting (see page 8).

STITCH

1. Begin at one of the center rows, bringing the bobbin thread to the top and stitching in place to create a starting knot (fig. B).

2. Stitch from left to right to create a row of loops (fig. C).

3. At the end of the row, stitch down to the next line and stitch a row of upside-down loops—this time stitching from right to left (fig. D). To end, stitch in place to create a knot.

4. Continue stitching, starting and stopping each row with a knot. Add scallops, double scallops, and offset scallops to create a new design (fig. E). Complete the exercise by stitching your signature and the date.

EVALUATE

+ Look carefully at your quilt sample. Did doodling before quilting help you plan your quilting and make your quilting line smoother?

+ Simple motifs can be transformed into beautiful patterns when combined in rows. What combination did you like the best? Would loops or scallops work on one of your current quilt tops?

+ Are your supplies organized so you can take advantage of small amounts of time to doodle or quilt?

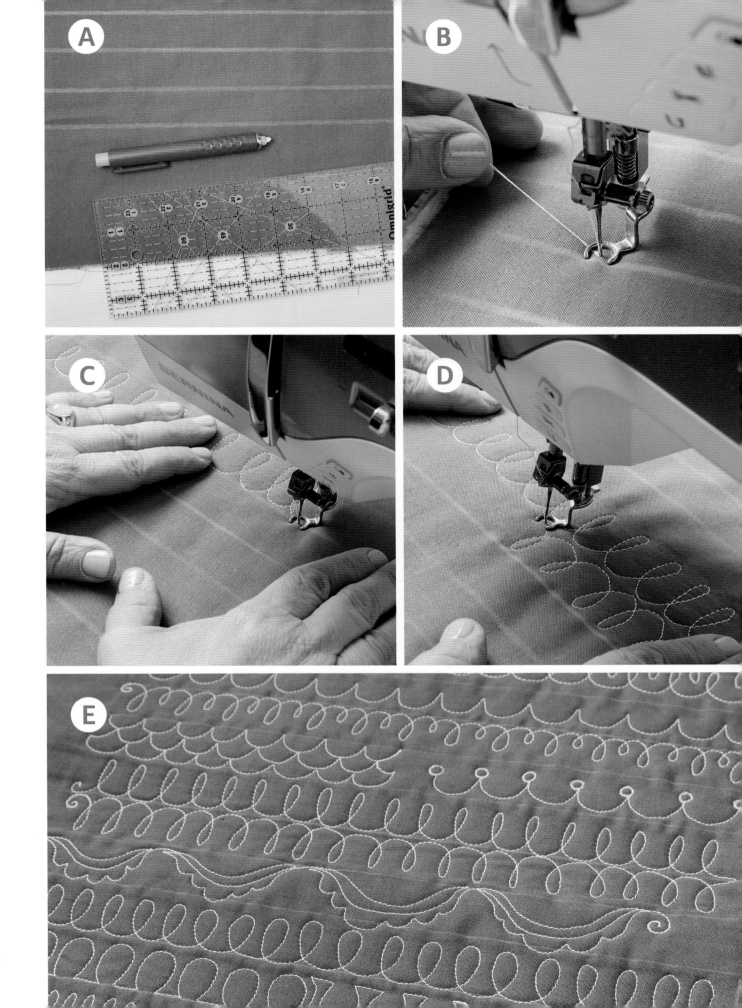

HAND POSITION AND NEEDLE DOWN

One of the fundamental skills of machine quilting is knowing how to maneuver the quilt under the needle to create beautiful motifs and patterns. Using good technique and proper hand position will allow you to control quilts of any size while remaining relaxed.

HAND POSITION

Learning good hand position will help you control the quilt to create a smooth stitching line. You need to control only a small area of the quilt at a time to create a motif. Stop frequently while quilting to adjust the quilt and plan the next area of quilting.

THE HOME POSITION

Place your hands on the quilt in an upside-down heart-shaped hoop position, with your thumbs 1" to 2" apart and your index fingers pointing slightly inward. Find a position that is relaxed and natural for your hands. This is your "home" position and your primary quilting area, where you have the most control of the quilt. If you try to stitch outside of your home position, you'll reduce your ability to control the quilt and the stitching line.

From your relaxed position, press down slightly with your thumb and fingertips and slide the quilt sandwich left and right, up and down, and at any angle. This is how you move the quilt under the needle. Your hands should always remain in the same comfortable position, with your fingers pointing away from you (fig. A).

AVOID THE STEERING WHEEL EFFECT

If you notice your fingers rotating to the left or right, and that your quilt is turning like a steering wheel (fig. B), stop and reposition your hands. You'll be more comfortable and have better control of the quilt if your hands always maintain the home position. You may feel the tendency to rotate your fingers, especially when stitching large, circular motifs. Practice keeping your hands in position as you move the quilt.

WHEN TO MOVE YOUR HANDS

Once you've stitched the area in your home position, you'll need to move your hands to stitch the next area. Stop stitching every time you move your hands. Stitching while moving your hands is like driving a car with your hands in the air—you'll likely crash, or in this case, create a jagged quilting line. You have poor control of the quilting line while moving your hands.

Needle Down

Most newer model sewing machines have a "needle-down" option, which is a great asset in free-motion quilting. With the needle-down feature engaged, every time you stop stitching, the needle will automatically stop in the down position, thereby holding your place within a motif. If this feature isn't available on your machine, practice timing stops with the needle down, or use the handwheel to lower the needle manually.

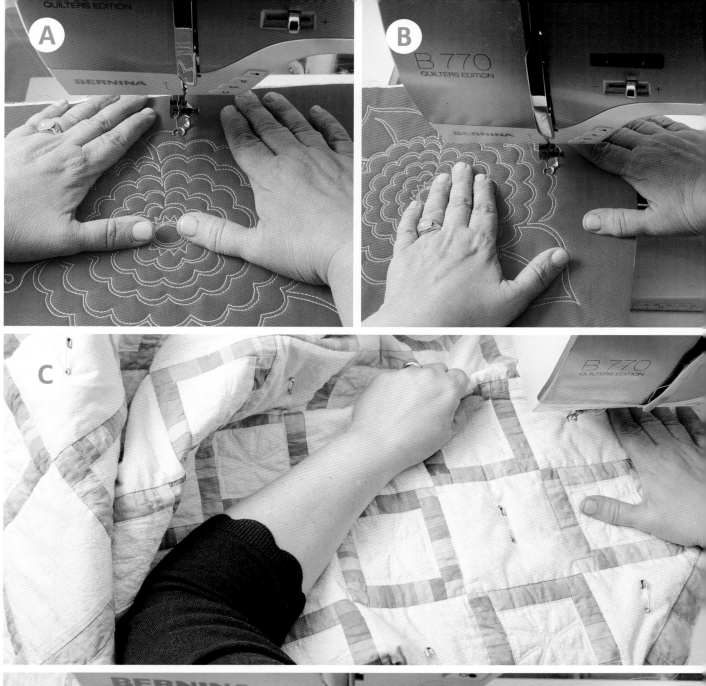

ELBOW AND FINGER PINCH METHOD

On some very large quilts, it may be necessary to position your left elbow on the bulk of the quilt to prevent the weight of the quilt from tugging and to help move the quilt while quilting. It may also help to pinch the layers of a large quilt with your left hand to gain better control (fig. C, page 27).

QUILT EDGES

Notice that when you near the edges of your quilt, you will only be able to fit one hand on the quilt. Consequently, you have less control of the quilt. For this reason, avoid quilting to the outer edges of your quilt sandwich while practicing (fig. D, page 27) and, if possible, add extra-wide batting and backing pieces for better gripping.

PRACTICE: THE MESSY SPIRAL POSY

In this practice session, focus on maintaining the home position as you stitch.

SUPPLIES

+ 1 quick quilt sandwich (page 14)
+ Top thread (heavyweight thread that contrasts well with the top fabric)
+ Bobbin thread (50-weight or lighter in a color that matches the top thread)

GET READY

1. Doodle Messy Spirals by circling clockwise and counterclockwise. Doodle leaves that are wide at the base.

2. Mark a 6" square in the center of the quilt sandwich. Add a 2"-wide border around the square.

3. Set up your machine for quilting (see page 8).

STITCH

Remember to stitch within your home position; don't steer! Practice stopping with the needle in the down position.

1. Starting in the center of the square, stitch a 1" to 2" circle (don't measure; just estimate).

2. Spiral clockwise into the center of the circle and counterclockwise out to create a Messy Spiral. Add several more spirals in a variety of sizes around the center circle to create a cluster (fig. E).

3. Add simple leaf shapes around the cluster (fig. F).

4. Stitch a wavy line around the marked chalk lines to create a border (fig. G).

5. Complete the exercise by stitching your signature and the date.

Stitch Wavy Lines

It's very challenging to stitch a long, straight line while free-motion quilting, but a wavy line often looks just as nice. If a straight line is important for your design, use a ruler foot and ruler to free-motion quilt the line or use a machine-guided technique with the feed dogs engaged and a walking foot.

EVALUATE

+ Look for small Vs in the stitching line. They usually appear when the quilt wasn't smoothed out at before stitching began or when the quilt was tugged by gravity.

+ Listen as you stitch. Are you able to maintain a consistent speed?

+ Are you able to grip the quilt well?

28

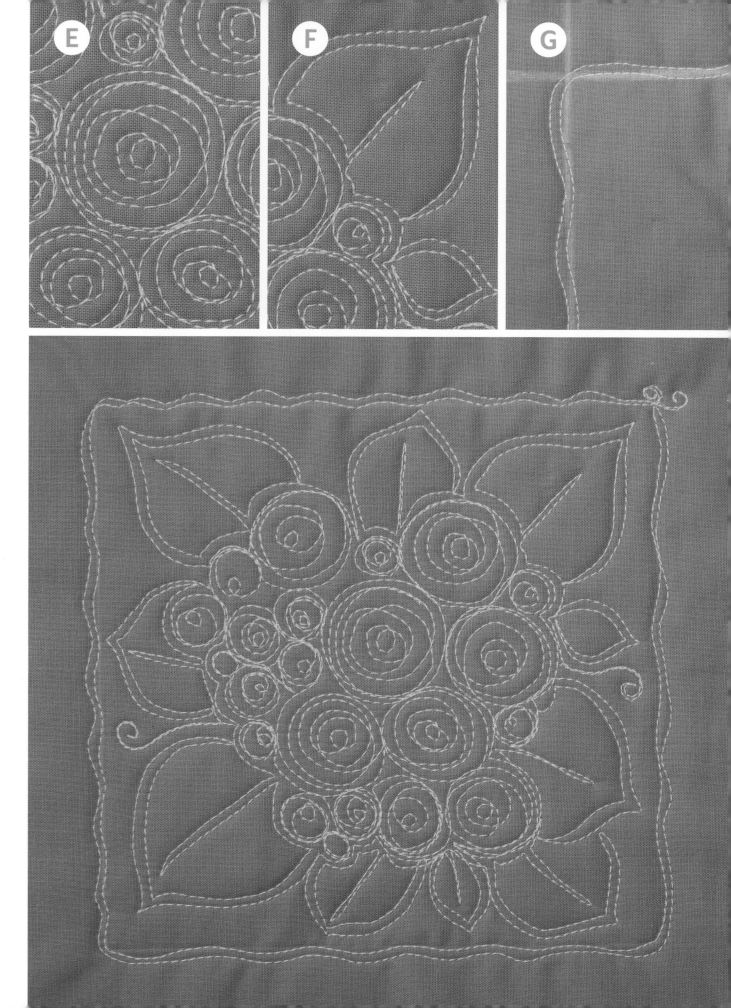

LESSON 6:

ADJUSTING YOUR MACHINE FOR THE PERFECT STITCH

One of the most important features of beautiful machine quilting is good stitch quality. The perfect stitch is a combination of proper stitch tension and pleasing stitch length.

BALANCED TENSION

The perfect stitch is well balanced and neither too tight nor too loose. A good quality stitch is balanced between the top and bobbin threads. In other words, the bobbin thread shouldn't peek out between the top stitches when viewed from the top of the quilt and the top thread shouldn't be visible on the back. Making a few machine adjustments can improve overall stitch quality. Remember to go through the "12-Step Setup for Free-Motion Quilting" (page 8) for excellent results (fig. A).

WHAT AFFECTS TENSION?

Many factors can affect stitch tension, including thread, batting, and fabric. Temperature and humidity can also influence sewing-machine tension. It's important to evaluate tension regularly and understand how to make machine adjustments in order to achieve beautiful quilting.

No matter how carefully you adjust your machine, there will be times when the stitches aren't balanced everywhere. Whenever possible, use the same thread color in the top and bobbin to avoid obvious tension imperfections.

ADJUSTING TENSION

For most sewing machines, adjusting only the top tension is enough to achieve a well-balanced stitch. In most cases, lowering or reducing the top tension is what's needed for machine quilting. Before adjusting bobbin tension, first check that your machine is cleaned and well-oiled and there are no stray threads or lint in the bobbin case. If you still feel the need to adjust the bobbin tension, use your machine manual as a guide.

Some sewing machines have a "finger" projection from the bobbin to help increase the bobbin tension. Thread this while free-motion quilting to help create a balanced tension.

FINDING THE BEST TENSION

When the top thread tension is too high, the bobbin thread is visible on top of the quilt. Lower the top tension one step or number at a time until the bobbin thread is no longer visible on the quilt top.

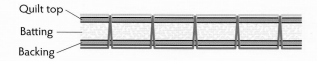

When the top thread tension is too low, the top thread is visible on the back of the quilt. Increase the top tension one step or number at a time until the top thread is no long visible on the quilt back.

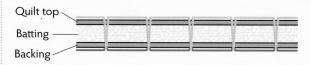

In perfect tension, the bobbin thread doesn't show on the top of the quilt, and the top thread doesn't show on the back of the quilt.

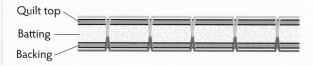

31

PRACTICE: ADJUSTING TENSION FOR THE PERFECT STITCH

In this practice session, you'll try different sewing-machine settings to find the optimal tension setting.

SUPPLIES

+ 1 quick quilt sandwich (page 14)

+ Top thread (heavyweight thread that contrasts well with the top fabric)

+ Bobbin thread (50-weight or lighter in a color that matches the top thread)

+ Single-hole throat plate

GET READY

1. Doodle on paper for five minutes. Create short wavy lines. Try some with rounded corners and a few with pointed corners. Add stars, circles, or other shapes.

2. Use white chalk and a ruler to mark horizontal lines 1" apart on the top fabric of the quilt sandwich.

3. Set up your machine for quilting.

STITCH

1. Create a starting knot by holding the top and bobbin threads taut while you stitch in place.

2. Stitch a short wavy line from left to right and back again. Look at your stitches.

3. Lower the top tension slightly and stitch again. Check your stitches.

4. Lower the tension again and stitch another wavy line to the right and back again.

5. Continue stitching wavy lines (fig. B). As you quilt, adjust your stitches to see how far you can lower your top tension. Lower the top tension as low as it will go. What happens? Many modern sewing machines have excellent tension control; other machines do not stitch well when the tension is set too low.

6. Remove your quilt from the sewing machine and check the back. Evaluate the stitch quality. Which stitching lines look the best?

7. Set your machine to the tension that looked best. Return the quilt to the sewing machine and begin stitching wavy lines again. Stitch any of your doodles. Follow the marked lines or stitch outside of the lines. Stitch vertical wavy lines away from yourself and then toward yourself (fig. C).

8. Complete the exercise by stitching stars and more doodles to your wavy lines (fig. D). Stitch your signature and the date (fig. E). Save this quilt sandwich to test your tension. Test tension before every project and every time you change threads.

EVALUATE

+ Does your machine have a sweet spot? Make a mental note of your tension numbers, but it's more important to know what a good stitch looks like and how to make the necessary adjustments to create it.

+ Examine your stitches to develop an eye for what the perfect stitch looks like.

+ Listen to your machine as you stitch. Pay attention to how it sounds when it's well-oiled and has a new needle. Any change in that sound probably means some maintenance is required.

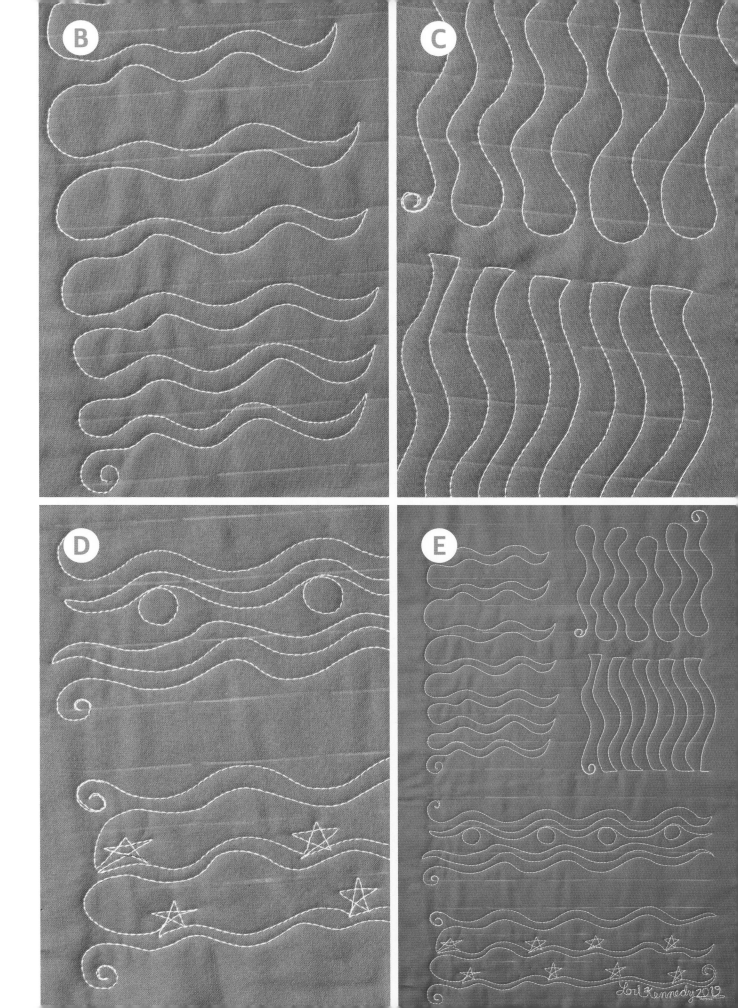

Lori Kennedy 2019

LESSON 7:

THE PERFECT STITCH LENGTH

The perfect stitch is a combination of balanced tension and pleasant-looking stitch length, with each stitch visible. The proper stitch length is subjective and may vary depending on the motifs, style of the quilt, and thickness of the batting. Keep in mind, good stitch formation is more important than perfect motifs.

PRACTICE

Achieving even stitch length (fig. A) requires good timing between your hand movement and machine speed. Coordinating the speed of your hands and the machine takes regular practice. To develop your skill, start with small projects that you can move easily under the needle before advancing to larger projects. Doodling helps by creating fluency and muscle memory.

EVEN SPEED

Quilting is like driving a car. It's important to maintain a smooth ride. Avoid lurching from slow speeds to fast speeds or everyone will get whiplash! Listen to the sound of your machine as you stitch. Your machine should whir at one consistent sound. If you hear it going faster or slower, your quilting will be more difficult and your stitch length will be uneven. While stitching, try to keep an even tempo with your hands and foot pedal. Maintain an even speed with the foot pedal and time the movement of the quilt to keep pace.

TROUBLESHOOTING

+ **Stitches are too long** (fig. B). Move the quilt slower or increase the needle speed (faster on the gas pedal).

+ **Stitches are too short** (fig. C). Move the quilt faster or decrease the needle speed (slower on the gas pedal).

+ **Stitches are uneven,** some short and some long (fig. D). Doodle more. Stitch with an even speed, letting your hands keep pace. Practice!

STOPPING AND STARTING

Stop with the needle in the down position every time you reposition your hands, adjust your quilt, or plan where to stitch next. As you resume stitching, it can be difficult to maintain a smooth starting line, so whenever possible, stop stitching in an inconspicuous spot where the stitching line changes direction, such as the inner points on the flower petals (fig. E). Avoid stopping in the middle of a smooth line.

Each time you begin stitching again, make sure the quilt is smooth and say out loud, "Ready, quilt!" Verbalizing helps you focus as you begin stitching. After some practice, you'll no longer need the words. Your timing will become automatic.

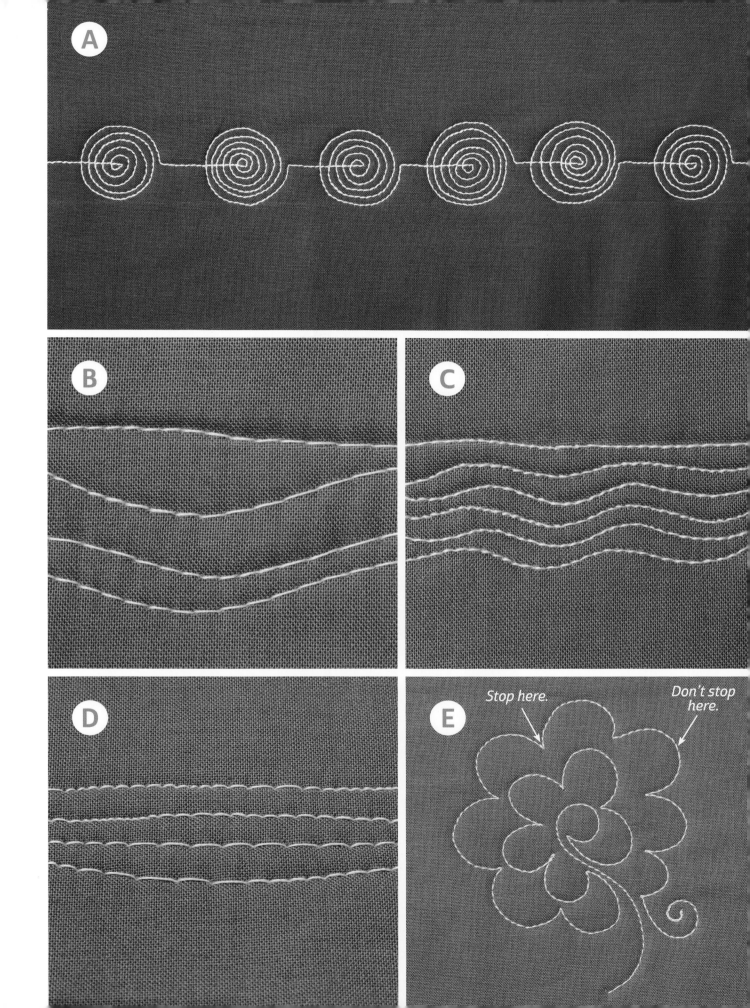

DEVELOP YOUR BEST SPEED

It takes frequent practice to develop your sense of timing. Don't be discouraged! The "Fast/Slow Exercise" below right will help you find a good quilting speed. Repeat this exercise regularly as a quilting warm-up. It may seem logical that slower is better, but most often, forcing ourselves to stitch a little faster than we're used to creates a smoother quilting line.

PRACTICE: SPIRALS AND LINE GRID

In this practice session, you'll work on maintaining an even stitch length.

DOODLE

Doodle for five minutes. Draw clockwise and counterclockwise circle scribbles. Doodle wavy lines horizontally and vertically and be sure to practice your signature and date. Add any of your favorite doodles.

SUPPLIES

+ 1 quick quilt sandwich (page 14)
+ Top thread (heavyweight thread that contrasts well with the top fabric)
+ Bobbin thread (50-weight or lighter in a color that matches the top thread)

GET READY

Use white chalk and a ruler to draw an 8 × 8 grid, spacing the lines 2" apart, on the top fabric of the quilt sandwich (fig. F). Set up your machine for quilting (see page 8).

STITCH

1. Test the tension in the margin of the quilt sandwich (see lesson 6 on page 30).

2. Starting in the upper-left square, create a starting knot (page 54). Stitch vertical wavy lines (fig. G).

3. In the next square, stitch horizontal wavy lines (fig. H). Continue stitching wavy lines, changing directions from horizontal to vertical, as you move from square to square.

4. Add a Messy Spiral (page 28) or one of your favorite doodles to add design interest (fig. I). Try the fast/slow exercise below.

5. As you stitch, listen carefully to the sound of your machine and try to keep an even speed. Be aware of your natural speed, then try to stitch a little faster. Complete the small quilt by filling in all of the squares. Add your signature and the date.

FAST/SLOW EXERCISE

1. Stitch at your normal speed for one minute.

2. Stitch very slowly for one minute.

3. Stitch very fast for one minute.

4. Stitch at any comfortable speed for one minute.

5. Think about it: which is harder—very fast or very slow? Did you find a "new normal" speed?

EVALUATE

+ Check for areas in your quilting where the stitches are uneven.

+ How do you feel when you are stitching? Are you relaxed or tense?

+ Watch for small Vs that indicate the quilt was being pulled when sewing started.

+ How would Messy Spirals and line quilting (fig. J) look on one of your quilts?

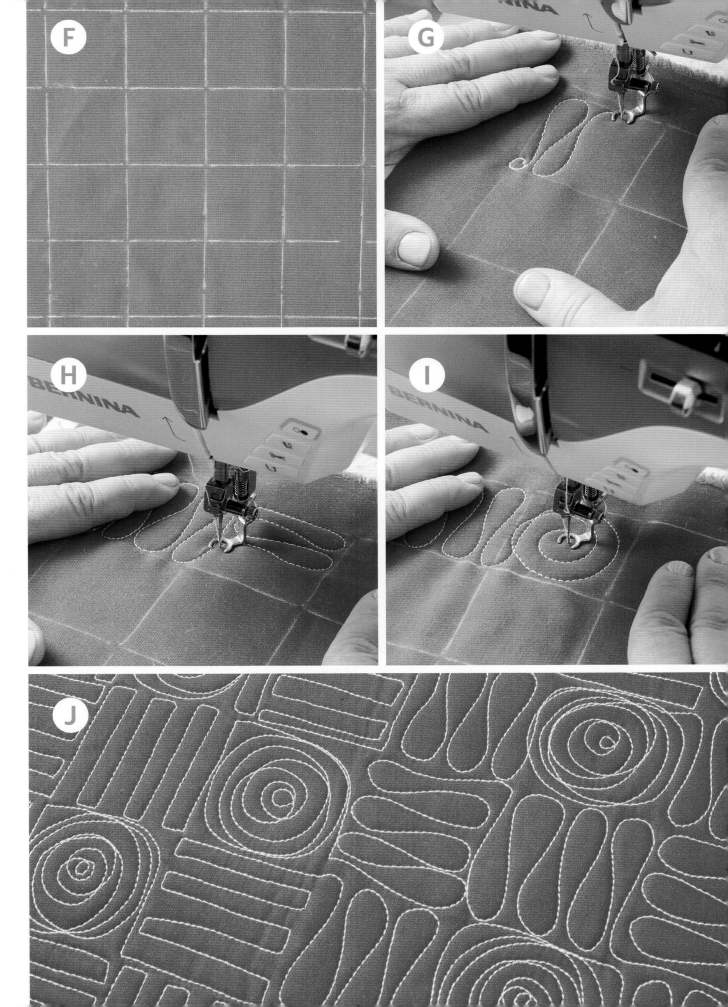

FOUR FUN MOTIFS

Choosing motifs is one of the most satisfying aspects of machine quilting. A motif can be subtle, to emphasize piecing or appliqué, or it can be the life of the party, adding a design to a plain border or block. Choose motifs that add personality to your quilts and enhance the style and theme. While the choice of motifs is endless, it's a good idea to start with a few tried and true motifs. Here we'll learn the Silly Spiral, Twist, Flower Power, and Square Flower.

SILLY SPIRAL

Spirals are whimsical circles that can stand alone or be used as the center of a flower. Stitch a single row of Silly Spirals to fill a border or stitch offset rows of spirals to fill a block or background.

Doodle the Silly Spiral motif by drawing a short line and then drawing a circle clockwise or counterclockwise over the line. To move to the next spiral, add a straight line in any direction and add more spirals.

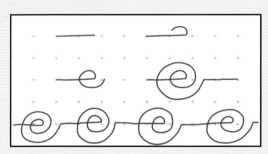

TWIST

The Twist is one of my favorite motifs because it can be squished or stretched to fill almost any shape. It's quick to stitch because it has rhythm. In other words, this motif rocks back and forth without stopping. The Twist is formed by connecting familiar figure-eight shapes. Practice by doodling figure eights. Once you get started, you won't want to stop!

To doodle the design, draw three parallel guidelines. Starting near the middle line, draw a counterclockwise upward loop to the top line, travel down, and then draw a clockwise downward loop to the bottom line. Try to keep the loops perpendicular to the guidelines.

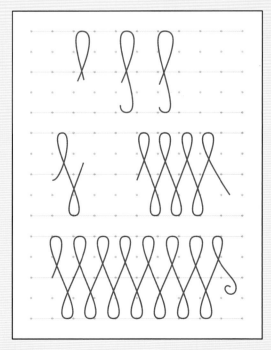

FLOWER POWER

This pretty posy is a versatile motif that's very easy to stitch and looks great when stitched large or small. A single flower can fill a square or connect many flowers in an allover design to quickly cover an entire quilt. To keep the stitching line neat, stitch rows of petals clockwise and counterclockwise without stitching over the stem.

To fill a block with Flower Power, draw a small stem with a curl in the center of the shape. Add one or many rows of scallops around the flower, stretching the petals to fill the square's corners.

To create an allover pattern, draw a short, curved stem with a small circle on top. Add scallops around the center. Reverse to add additional rows of scallops. Continue adding rows of scallops to create any flower size. Add another short stem to begin another flower.

SQUARE FLOWER

The Square Flower is a charming way to fill any square block and can be easily modified to fill other shapes. It looks great in the plain square blocks found in many quilt patterns and it combines well with the Twist (page 38).

To doodle, first draw a square. Draw a spiral in the center of the square. Draw a petal to the top of the square and back down. Draw a second petal angling into the corner of the square. Continue adding petals clockwise around the flower.

Corner Motifs

When stitching some border motifs, the transition corner from horizontal to vertical can be challenging. To avoid a messy corner, use a transition motif like the Silly Spiral or Square Flower.

40

PRACTICE THE MOTIFS

In this practice session, you'll stitch the Flower Power and Square Flower motifs.

DOODLE THE MOTIFS

Practice drawing the two floral motifs. Repeat the motifs many times (over time, it can be helpful to doodle motifs hundreds of times) until both motifs flow easily on paper.

SUPPLIES

+ 1 quick quilt sandwich (page 14)*
+ Top thread (heavyweight thread that contrasts well with the top fabric)
+ Bobbin thread (50-weight or lighter in a color that matches the top thread)

If you'd like to eventually turn this piece into a longer table runner, adjust the size of your quilt sandwich accordingly.

GET READY

1. Draw two vertical parallel lines spaced 4" apart through the center of the top fabric of the quilt sandwich. Divide the space into five 4" squares (or more for a longer table runner). Add a 1"-wide border on both sides of the squares. Mark an additional 1½"-wide border on both sides.

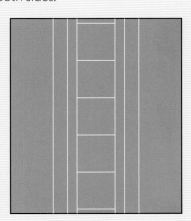

2. Set up your machine for quilting (see page 8).

STITCH

1. In the margins of the quilt, practice the motifs and test your tension.

2. Create a starting knot by holding the top and bobbin threads taut while you stitch in place. Stitch a slightly wavy line over the long, vertical marked lines on the quilt. Starting at the same end each time, stitch all the vertical lines first, knotting off between each line. (This will keep the layers from shifting and the quilt from distorting.) **Tip:** Long straight lines are the most difficult shape to free-motion quilt. Whenever your design allows, stitch a slightly wavy line instead of a straight line or switch to machine-guided or ruler-work quilting.

3. Starting at either short end, stitch the horizontal lines. Do not knot off between the short lines. Instead, travel to the next line by closely echo stitching the vertical lines (fig. A).

4. Alternate stitching Square Flower and Flower Power (figures B, C, and D) in each of the squares. Knot off between each of the flower motifs and change thread color if desired.

5. Save the sample for Lesson 9: A Smooth Glide (page 44).

EVALUATE

+ Do you have a few tried and true motifs?
+ How would Flower Power, Square Flower, Twist, or Silly Spirals look on one of your quilts?
+ Is there anyplace on your quilts where a slightly wavy line could replace a straight line?

42

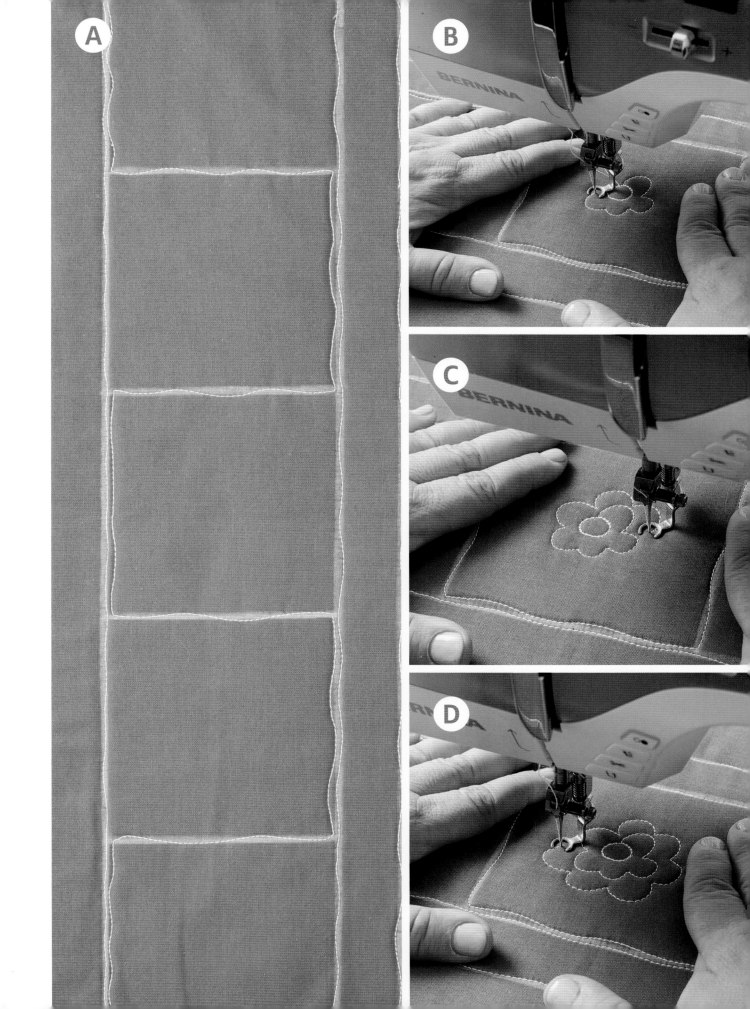

LESSON 9:

A SMOOTH GLIDE

Once the feed dogs are lowered for free-motion quilting, the sewing machine no longer controls the speed and direction of the stitching line—you do! In this lesson, you'll evaluate your work space to learn ways to minimize the effects of gravity and friction so you can move your quilt freely.

Cabinets and extension tables. A machine set in a cabinet provides the largest work space and support and is ideal for machine quilting on a sewing machine. A less expensive option is to invest in an extension table (such as Sew Steady), which can be custom fit for most sewing-machine models. The additional support to the quilt helps reduce the effect of gravity and provides a larger work space for maneuvering the quilt. Alternatively, you can stack boxes and books around your machine to create a makeshift extension table.

Sewing studio layout. To support a very large quilt, it's helpful to place ironing boards or banquet tables both behind and to the left of the sewing machine. If possible, set up the sewing tables in the corner of a room against the walls to prevent the quilt from sliding off the tables and tugging the quilt while you are stitching.

Reducing friction. Free-motion quilting is easier when you take steps to help the quilt move freely under the needle. The Supreme Slider is a self-sticking sheet that sits over the bed of the sewing machine and reduces the effects of friction, which allows the quilt to glide more readily. The Supreme Slider comes in several sizes. Use the largest size that fits on your sewing-machine table. Some quilters tape the slider in place with painter's tape to be sure it stays put during quilting (fig. A).

Smooth backing fabric. Avoid backing fabric with textured surfaces. Also, starch the backing fabric to improve glide while stitching (fig. B).

PRACTICE: MINIMIZING FRICTION

In this practice session, you'll evaluate ways to achieve a smooth glide as you quilt, using the sample from Lesson 8: Four Fun Motifs (page 38).

SUPPLIES

+ Quilt sandwich from lesson 8
+ Top thread (heavyweight thread that contrasts well with the top fabric)
+ Bobbin thread (50-weight or lighter in a color that matches the top thread)
+ Supreme Slider (optional)
+ Spray starch (optional)

DOODLE

Place the vinyl overlay you made in Lesson 3: Start a Doodle Habit (page 19) on top of the sample from lesson 8. Doodle Silly Spirals between the marked 1"-wide lines and Twist between the marked 1½"-wide lines to test the scale of each motif (fig. C).

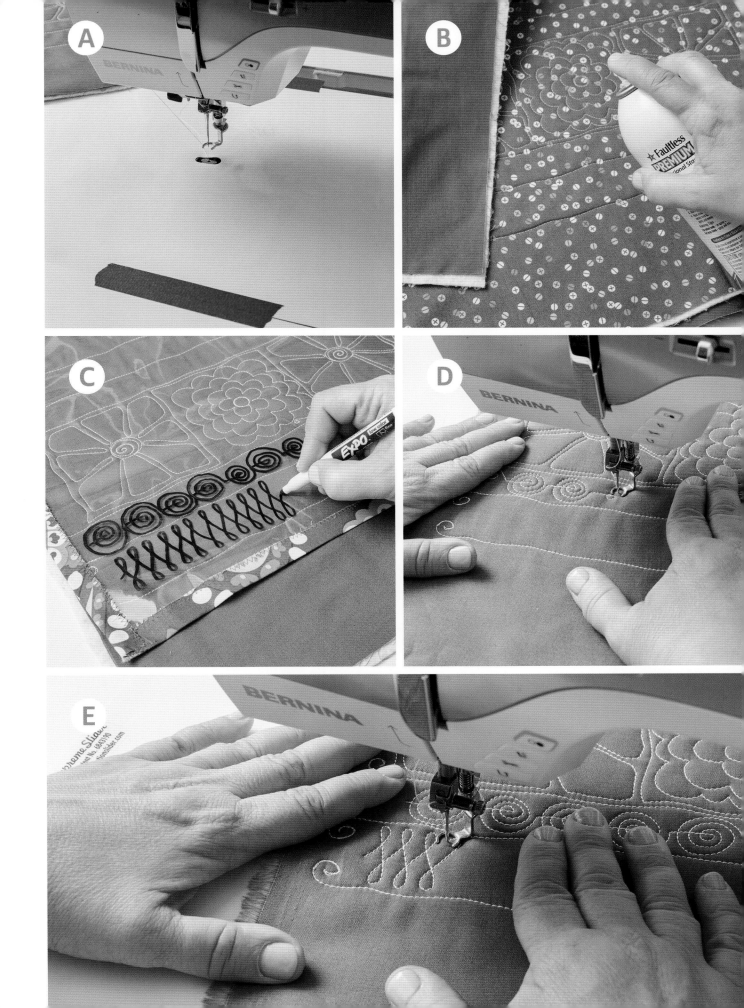

GET READY

1. Set up your machine for quilting (see page 8).

2. Starch the backing fabric and tape a Supreme Slider in place (optional).

> ### Test: Starching the Backing Fabric
>
> 1. *Create a quick quilt sandwich without starching the backing fabric.*
>
> 2. *Stitch any motif for several minutes and notice how the quilt moves.*
>
> 3. *Remove the quilt from the sewing machine, then starch and press the back of the quilt sandwich.*
>
> 4. *Continue quilting and notice whether or not starching helps reduce friction for a smoother glide.*

STITCH

1. Stitch Silly Spirals in the 1"-wide border (fig. D, page 45).

2. Stitch Twist in the 1½"-wide border (fig. E, page 45).

3. Complete the exercise by stitching your signature and the date.

EVALUATE

✦ Place a large quilt or quilt top under your needle. Move the quilt around as if you were quilting. Does the quilt drop off the work surface?

✦ Would rearranging your sewing room allow you to support quilts better?

LESSON 10:

DIRECTIONAL STITCHING

Which way should you stitch a motif? Right to left? Left to right?
From the bottom up or from the top down? The answer is, it depends!
Let's explore options in directional stitching.

STITCHING DIRECTION

Four factors determine the direction of stitching: natural preference, field of view, quilt size, and the motif.

Natural Preference. Most quilters prefer to quilt from left to right. After years of writing from left to right, the most natural way to quilt is also from left to right because we have built-in muscle memory. Choose left to right stitching whenever possible.

Greatest Field of View. It's easier to quilt when you can see where you're headed. Choose the direction that allows the greatest field of view. Stitching along a horizontal axis of the quilt, from left to right and back again, allows the greatest visibility because it allows you to see both where you're headed as well as where you've already quilted. When it's necessary to stitch on a vertical axis, stitching from the top down allows you to see where you're headed, whereas when stitching from the bottom up, the field of view is partially blocked by the needle and presser foot. Choose horizontal or top-down stitching for the greatest field of view.

Quilt Size. When stitching a small quilt, take advantage of the size to rotate the quilt in whichever position makes it easiest to stitch. When stitching a large quilt, managing the bulk within the harp space (the work space underneath the arm of the machine) will dictate the position of the quilt and the direction of stitching. You'll need to practice stitching horizontally, vertically, and upside down (the quilt, not YOU!).

Directional Motifs. Quilt design may influence how you position the quilt while stitching. Some motifs, such as sailboats, are directional and it may feel more natural to stitch them horizontally (fig. A).

MAKE DIRECTIONAL STITCHING EASIER

The following techniques will help make directional stitching easier.

Choose the right foot. Most sewing-machine manufacturers offer several presser feet suitable for machine quilting. Choose the foot that allows the greatest visibility. Presser feet that are open-toed and offset offer the greatest field of view. (See step 3 of lesson 2 on page 16.)

Stop and Look. While it may seem obvious, stop frequently to check where you are headed and estimate spacing.

Use tactile clues. When stitching vertically from the bottom up, extend your index finger just beyond where you plan to create a stitching line. Your finger will add a tactile clue to stitch into the blind spot beyond the needle (fig. B).

Doodle. Doodling creates muscle memory and is extremely beneficial for quilting motifs in any direction. Look at your quilt and determine which

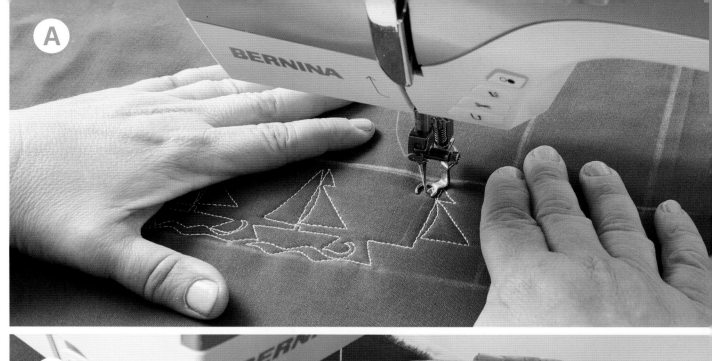

direction you'll need to stitch each motif. Practice doodling motifs horizontally, vertically, and upside down before stitching.

Draw first. If the position of the quilt dictates a stitching line that feels unnatural, it may help to draw the motif on the quilt and then follow the line. For example, it might be easier to follow a drawn border of sailboats than to stitch it from memory upside down or sideways, when the quilt cannot be rotated easily (fig. C, page 49).

PRACTICE: SUNNY DAY MEDALLION QUILT

In this practice session, you'll try both machine-guided and free-motion directional stitching. But first, we'll doodle the designs.

DOODLE

1. Practice doodling motifs from left to right and from right to left. Create a sun motif by doodling a spiral with small triangles around the edges.

2. Doodle motifs like Twist and Silly Spirals vertically and horizontally to fill the borders. Add other motifs like Messy Spirals and straight-line quilting.

3. Dots and Dashes are a great stepping stone to learning more complex motifs like Pearls and Pebbles. Doodle a short straight line. Add a clockwise circle, 1½ revolutions. Add another short dash and a counterclockwise circle.

4. To create Pearls, combine clockwise and counterclockwise circles without the dash in between. To create Pebbles, doodle a cluster of clockwise and counterclockwise circles in different sizes.

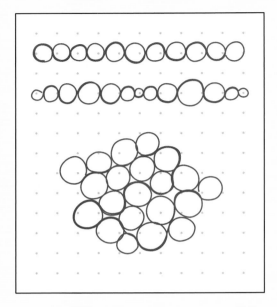

SUPPLIES

+ 1 quick quilt sandwich (page 14)*

+ Top thread (heavyweight thread that contrasts well with the top fabric)

+ Bobbin thread (50-weight or lighter in a color that matches the top thread)

If you'd like to eventually turn this piece into a longer table runner, adjust the size of your quilt sandwich accordingly.

GET READY

1. Set up your machine for quilting (see page 8).

2. Starch the backing if you found it helped your quilt glide more smoothly in lesson 9.

3. Use white chalk and a ruler to mark a 6" square in the center on the top fabric of the quilt sandwich. Mark a 1"-wide border around the square. Then mark a 1½"-wide border to create a medallion style composition.

STITCH

As you stitch, remember to maintain your "home" position with your hands, and avoid the steering-wheel effect.

1. Set your machine for machine-guided sewing with the feed dogs engaged. If you have a walking foot, use or engage it to keep the layers of the quilt from shifting.

2. Stitch on the marked lines to outline each square. Notice that with machine-guided stitching, in order to change the direction of the stitching line, you must rotate the quilt. For a small quilt, rotating the quilt is easy. However, when stitching a large quilt, it's usually easier to stitch free-motion style to avoid rotating the quilt.

3. Set up your machine for free-motion quilting. Lower the feed dogs and change the thread to a color that contrasts with the fabric. Stitch a sun motif in the center. Stitch Silly Spirals or Dots and Dashes in the 1"-wide border. In the 1½"-wide border, stitch Twist with a spiral in each corner.

4. Stitch the border motifs without rotating the quilt: Stitch the top border from left to right and the right border vertically from top to bottom. Then stitch the bottom border from right to left and the left border vertically from the bottom to the top.

5. Complete the exercise by stitching your signature and the date.

EVALUATE

+ Which direction of stitching was easiest for you?

+ What made it easier—natural preference, field of view, directional motif, or quilt size?

+ Which direction was most challenging?

+ Did you prefer machine-guided or free-motion outlines?

Personalize Every Quilt

One of the great advantages of doing our own quilting is that it gives us the opportunity to add personal details to our quilts. In addition to choosing quilting motifs with character, I love to use my "handwriting" to leave messages within the quilting lines.

Practice doodling continuous-line letters. To create the letters *i* and *j*, add the dot just after you complete the upward sweep of the letter. Cross the *t* and *x* as you make the letter to create a continuous line. Add a wavy line to separate words in a sentence.

Add favorite quotes, family jokes, song lyrics, and short prayers to your quilts using your handwriting. Your handwriting will elevate your projects from basic quilts to family heirlooms, and the messages will be love letters to future generations!

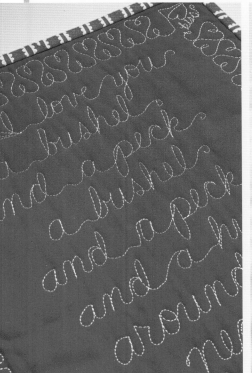
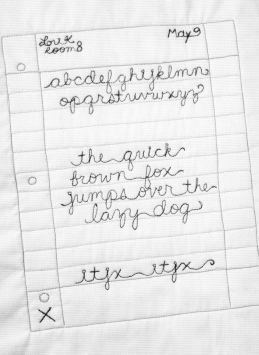

53

LESSON 11:

KNOTS

For every stitching line there are at least two knots, a starting knot and a stopping knot. If the thread breaks there may be a third knot, a repair knot. The knot you choose is determined by how much time you want to spend hiding the knot. For a quick knot, try my curlicue knot or design your own version.

QUILTING KNOTS

All of the following knots, when made correctly, hold up well to normal quilt use.

Stitch-in-place knot. The stitch-in-place knot is a quick knot created by machine stitching three or four tiny stitches over one another in a very short space (fig. A). The top and bobbin threads are trimmed as close to the quilt as possible. (Note: Some machine models create knots and cut the threads automatically. Check your owner's manual.) When stitched with lightweight thread, this knot is barely noticeable, but when stitched with heavyweight thread, the stitch-in-place knot can create an undesired focal point.

Hand-tied and buried knot. The hand-tied knot is the one to use for quilting competitions, as it's invisible. It's also the most time-consuming. Create this knot by leaving long bobbin and top thread tails at the beginning and end of each stitching line. Pull the top thread to the back and tie the threads together in a square knot. Thread the tails into a hand-sewing needle and bury the knot in the batting layer. Use a self-threading needle for faster knotting.

Curlicue knot. The curlicue knot takes advantage of the mini focal point created when several stitches are made on top of one another. Instead of stitching in place, stitch a small curly line and stitch over it to create a beginning and ending knot (fig. B). The result is a quilt punctuated by small curlicues. If curlicues do not fit your design, create a different pattern with overstitched lines. A simple leaf or triangle can be overstitched to create a different design element.

Surgeon's knot for repairs. The surgeon's knot is a variation of the hand-tied and buried knot and is done when the bobbin or top thread breaks during stitching, leaving a short tail. To make a surgeon's knot, pinch the short thread with a pair of tweezers. Wrap the long thread around the tweezers two or more times and pull the short thread through the loops. Bury the knot with a hand-sewing needle.

CUTTING THE BOBBIN THREAD

When stitching a large quilt, you may want to knot off and move to another section of the quilt to continue stitching. It is difficult to remove the entire bulk of the quilt and turn it over to snip the bobbin thread. You could cut the top thread and leave the bobbin thread intact as you move to the new position; however, doing so leaves a very long tail stretched across the back of the quilt. Another option is to cut the bobbin thread by pulling it to the top before moving the quilt.

1. Create a stitch-in-place or curlicue knot.

2. Raise the needle and the presser foot to release the tension (fig. C).

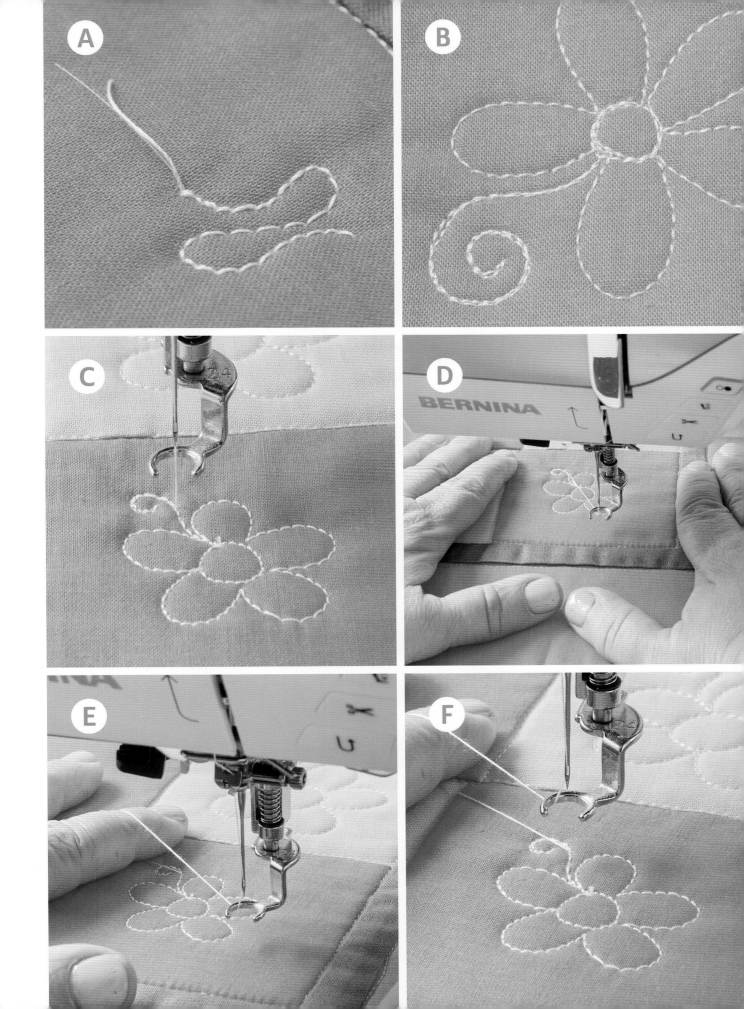

3. Slide the quilt several inches away from you to create slack in the bobbin thread (fig. D, page 55.)

4. Hold the top thread taut with your left hand (fig. E, page 55).

5. Reposition the quilt so the needle is directly over the knot (fig. F, page 55).

6. Lower the presser foot, then lower the needle and bring it back up again (fig. G).

7. Raise the presser foot and give the top thread a sharp tug; then use your tweezers to bring the bobbin thread to the top (fig. H).

8. Cut the thread and move the quilt to the new position to begin stitching again.

PRACTICE: MACHINE-TIED NINE PATCH

In this practice session, you'll make three types of knots: stitch-in-place, curlicue, and hand-tied.

DOODLE

Continue to practice doodling directional motifs. Doodle small curls and trace back over the line like you are creating a curlicue knot. Create variations of the Flower Power motif by changing the shape of the petals and ending with a curlicue knot.

SUPPLIES

+ 1 quick quilt sandwich (page 14)*

+ Top thread (lightweight thread that matches the top fabric and heavyweight thread that contrasts well with the background fabric)

+ Bobbin thread (50-weight or lighter in a color that matches the top thread)

If you have time, piece a Nine Patch quilt (any size) with a 2"-wide border around the block. Layer with batting and backing to make a quilt sandwich.

GET READY

1. Use white chalk and a ruler to mark a nine-patch grid with a 2"-wide border on the top fabric of the quilt sandwich. If using a Nine Patch quilt, omit this step.

2. Set up your machine for quilting (see page 8).

STITCH

1. Using lightweight thread, stitch a slightly wavy line over the marked lines of the nine-patch grid and border. Stitch a small motif in the center of four of the marked squares (top, bottom, and side center squares). Begin each line of stitching with a stitch-in-place knot and end each line with a curlicue knot. Between each motif, cut the bobbin thread by bringing it to the top.

2. Switch to a heavyweight thread and change the needle size. Add a motif to each of the remaining squares. Begin each line of stitching with a stitch-in-place knot and end each line with a curlicue knot. Between each motif, bring the bobbin thread to the top to cut it.

3. Complete the exercise by stitching your signature and the date, leaving a long tail at the beginning and end of the stitching line. Hand tie and bury the knots.

EVALUATE

+ Compare the stitch-in-place knots created with light and heavyweight threads.

+ Compare the curlicue knots created with light and heavyweight threads.

+ Think about your quilting style. Which knot are you most likely to use?

+ Will you use a different knot for different quilts?

+ Will you use different knots for different threads?

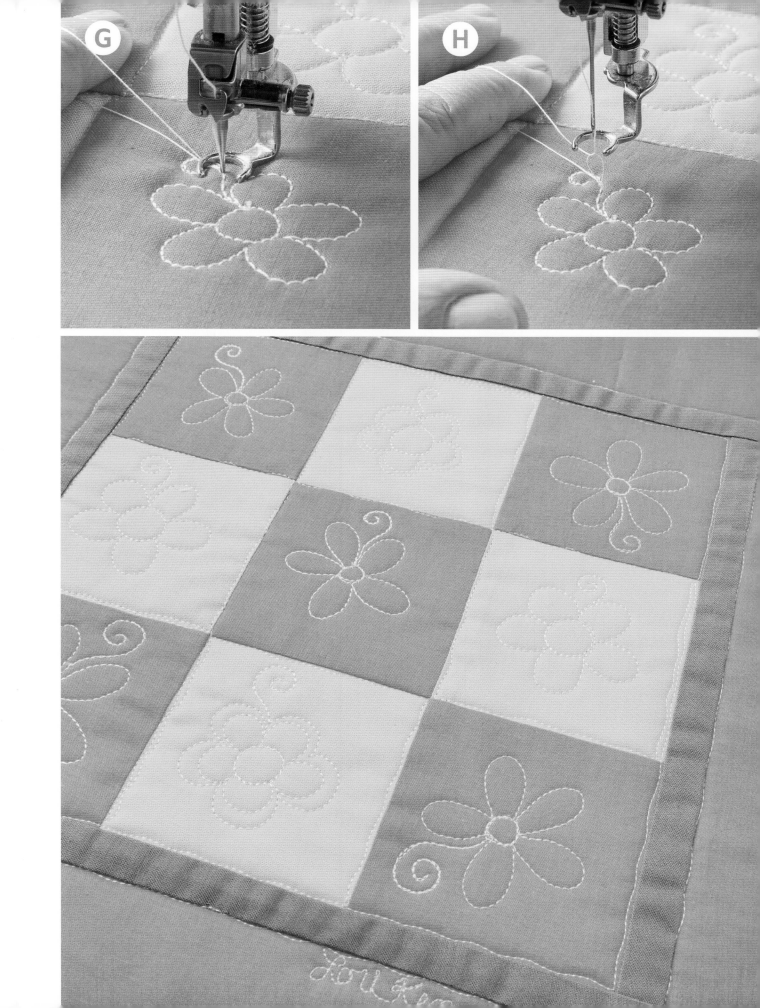

LESSON 12:

THREAD MATTERS

One of the fastest ways to improve the look of your quilting is to use the right thread. Throughout the rest of the lessons, sample a wide variety of threads to create custom quilting effects. First, let's reorganize your current thread stash and look at the properties of threads that determine how they will look on your quilts.

THREAD

Learning about thread is both challenging and rewarding. Thread labels are filled with abbreviations and every manufacturer has its own coding system. Furthermore, no industry standard exists, so there is no consistency across brands. However, understanding the properties of thread is richly rewarding because thread can instantly change the way your motifs and quilts look, for better or for worse!

Get in the habit of looking at thread by spooling out several inches and examining it closely. As you gain more quilting experience, you'll be able to predict how a thread will perform by inspecting the thread rather than relying on the label.

Beware of spools labeled "Quilting Thread." This wax-coated thread is designed for hand quilting and is not recommended for use in sewing machines.

THREAD CHARACTERISTICS

The type of fiber and how it's manufactured determines the strength, flexibility, weight, sheen, and color of the thread. Several fiber types are suitable for machine quilting (fig. A, page 61). Some popular thread fibers include cotton, polyester, rayon, silk, and wool. Each has different characteristics which can be used to create a variety of quilting effects. For example, rayon

and silk threads have a gorgeous sheen that reflects light while wool is fuzzy and adds interesting texture.

STRENGTH

Several factors help determine the best thread for any quilting project. Most importantly, the thread must be strong and flexible enough to quilt without breaking or shredding. Polyester and cotton threads are strong enough to be used as top and bobbin threads, while rayon is slightly weaker and should be used only as a top thread. If thread breaks or shreds while quilting, replace the needle and check for burrs around the throat plate or in the bobbin area. If problems persist, choose another thread.

WEIGHT

Thread weight impacts how a thread will look in the quilt. Thread weight is graded on a continuum from lightweight (or fine) to heavyweight. Lightweight thread has a higher number (100-weight) and heavyweight thread has a lower number (12-weight). Mediumweight (50-weight) thread is used for many sewing applications, including patchwork.

The weight of the thread is determined by the fiber type as well as how the thread was processed. Thread used for machine quilting can be one, two, or three ply, which refers to the number of single

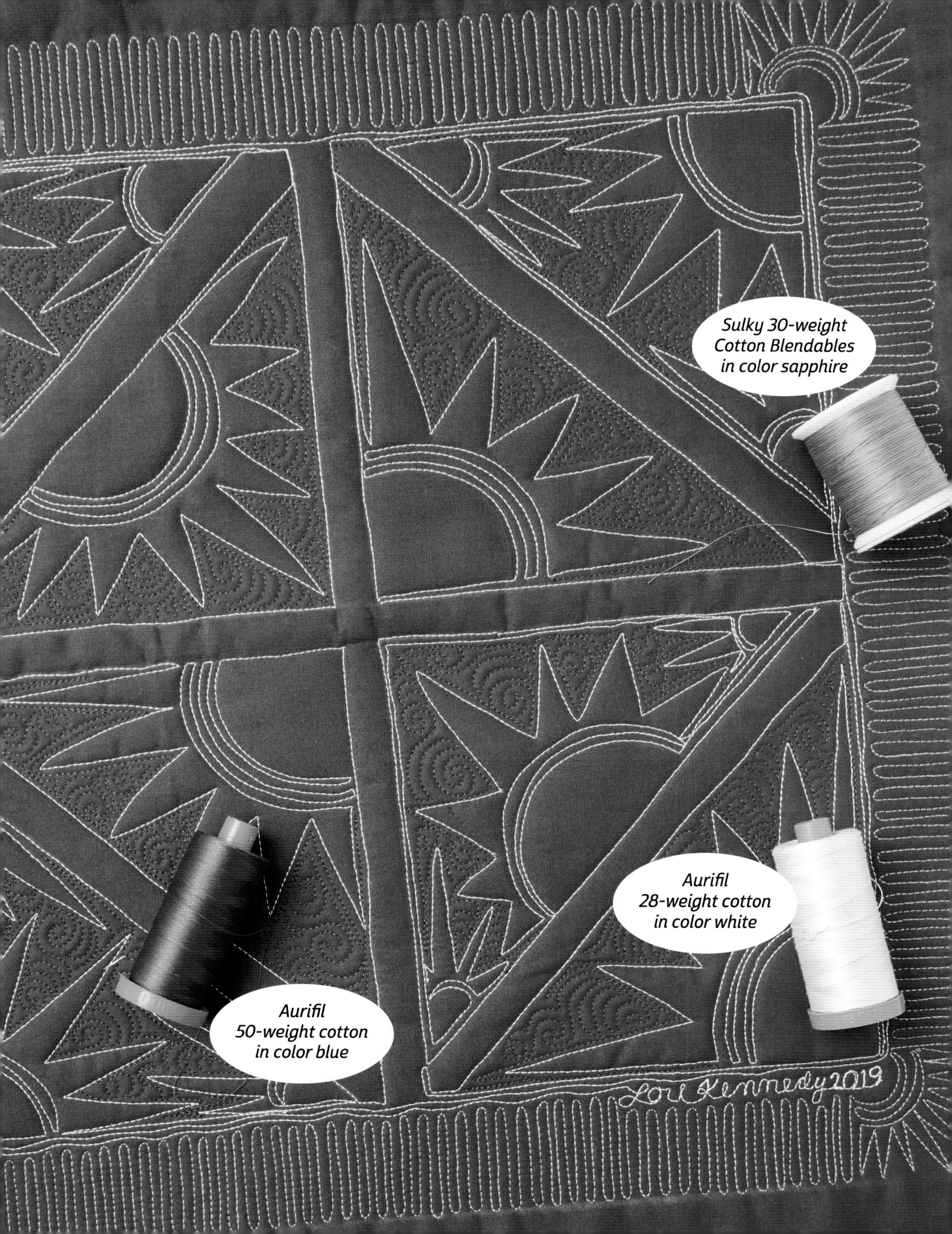

Sulky 30-weight
Cotton Blendables
in color sapphire

Aurifil
28-weight cotton
in color white

Aurifil
50-weight cotton
in color blue

Lori Kennedy 2019

fiber strands twisted together to create the thread. Thread weight is calculated differently by each manufacturer, so it's best to evaluate thread by inspection, rather than solely by reading the label.

FOCUS MOTIF OR TEXTURE ONLY?

Heavyweight thread is more likely to create a visible quilting design, whereas a lightweight thread will create subtler texture in a quilt. Consider the quilting effect you are trying to achieve before choosing the thread weight. For example, if you want to show off a quilted flower design, use heavyweight thread. On the other hand, if you want to show off elaborate piecing within the quilt top, use a lightweight thread to create texture only. Take another look at the stitched sun, where a heavier-weight thread is used on the sun and a lighter-weight thread is used for the border (fig. B).

BOBBIN THREAD

For most sewing applications, sewing-machine manufacturers recommend using the same thread in the top and bobbin to produce a balanced stitch. When quilting, however, it's best to use a strong, light- to mediumweight thread in the bobbin, regardless of the top thread. Bobbin thread should be strong, to minimize breakage, and thin, to maximize the amount of thread the bobbin can hold. Cotton and polyester are good choices. (Rayon does not have the tensile strength to be a good bobbin thread.) My favorite choice is 50-weight Aurifil cotton thread. It's a good balance between weight and strength and it has a slight sheen (fig. C).

It's best to match the color of the bobbin thread and the top thread. In that way, if the tension isn't perfect, the bobbin thread won't show through on the top of the quilt.

THREAD COLOR

Thread color is also important in quilt design. When you want to show off the quilting line or stitch a focal motif, choose a thread color that contrasts with the quilt fabric. To create texture, use a thread that matches or blends with the top fabric.

Choosing the best thread color can be challenging when stitching on heavily patterned fabric or pieced quilts, especially quilts with high-value contrast. One solution is to quilt with a medium-value thread. Many quilters choose medium-value gray, celery green, or purple for allover quilting. However, in order to achieve your design goals, you may have to change thread as you quilt over different-colored fabrics in the quilt.

ORGANIZE YOUR THREAD COLLECTION

Collect all of your thread in one place. Remove any thread that's old and set aside spools that no longer have a label. Sort your thread by weight into three categories light (or fine), medium, and heavyweight (fig. D).

WEIGHT CODING ON LABELS

Try to determine the weight by looking at the label. Look for the abbreviation "wt", or a number/2 or 3, for example 50/2, indicating weight over ply. Sometimes weight is labeled # or No., and some manufacturers, like Aurifil, include weight on the label and also use color-coded spools: gray is 28-weight and orange is 50-weight.

+ Lightweight thread is 100-, 80-, and 60-weight.

+ Mediumweight thread is 50- and 40-weight.

+ Heavyweight thread is 30-, 28-, and 12-weight.

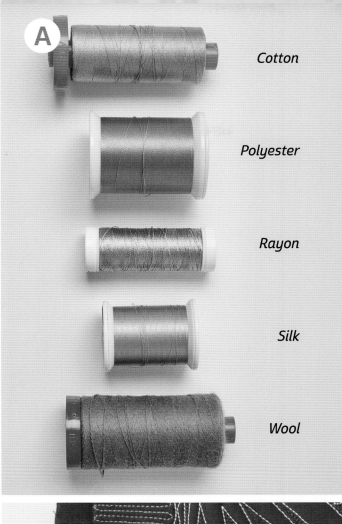

Cotton

Polyester

Rayon

Silk

Wool

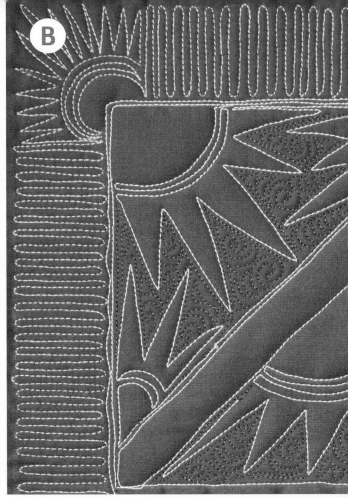

Instead of looking at the label, I use a more reliable method. Choose a 50-weight cotton thread and spool out a length of thread. Compare every thread in your collection to that thread and decide if it's heavier, lighter, or the same weight to create the weight categories.

FIBER CONTENT

For this lesson, only use threads made of cotton, polyester, and rayon. Set aside specialty threads like metallic or monofilament. Within each weight category, separate the thread into groups by fiber: cotton, polyester, and rayon.

Spool out several inches of each thread onto a piece of fabric as if you're auditioning it for a quilt. Run it through your fingers to feel the thread. Examine each thread more closely for the following properties.

Weight. Compare the thickness of the weights between and within a weight category: light, medium, and heavy.

Sheen. Sheen is the ability to reflect light. Some threads shine, while others have a duller finish.

Memory. Notice how the fiber falls off the spool. If the thread coils a lot, it's said to have memory and will likely be more challenging to stitch than fibers that lay flat as they unspool.

Feel. Run a length of thread between your fingers and note how it feels. Some threads are smooth and others have a noticeable texture. Some fibers are softer to the touch then others.

Color intensity. Some fibers absorb dye better than others so the colors appear more intense.

Fuzzy or smooth. Long staple fibers appear smoother than short staple threads that look fuzzy and produce more lint in your sewing machine.

COMPARE

Look at one weight group at a time. Compare brands and fibers. Look for similarities and differences. Within each weight group, see if you can tell the difference between the weights. For example, when looking at the lightweight threads, can you tell a difference between 60- and 80-weight thread? How does a lightweight cotton thread look and feel compared to a polyester thread? How do brands differ?

Repeat this process for each weight group. You might notice that some polyester threads feel and look similar to cotton thread and other polyester threads seem more like rayon thread. Notice how thread weight appears different across brands and fibers.

Make it a habit to examine your thread by spooling it out and feeling it before you begin stitching. After some practice, you'll be better at predicting how the thread will look when stitched. However, the only true way to test a thread is to quilt a sample!

Thread Weight vs. Needle Size

Heavyweight thread has a lower number because thread is measured using a fixed weight system. It's the length of thread necessary to achieve a fixed weight. Finer thread requires a longer length to achieve a given weight than a thicker thread.

Now here's where it gets confusing! As thread weight gets heavier, the number gets smaller, but as needle size gets larger, the number gets bigger!

The weight of the thread determines the size of the sewing-machine needle that should be used. Heavier threads require a larger needle and finer threads require a smaller needle. The smallest needle is 60/8 and the largest needle is 110/18. A great rule of thumb is to pair 50-weight thread with a size 80/12 needle. For heavier thread (28-weight), use a size 100/16 needle. For finer thread (80-weight), try a size 60/8 or 70/10 needle.

Broken thread, skipped stitches, or poor stitch formation may be a sign that the needle is the wrong size.

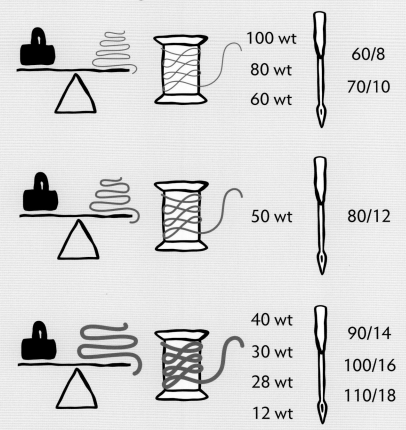

100 wt	60/8
80 wt	70/10
60 wt	
50 wt	80/12
40 wt	90/14
30 wt	100/16
28 wt	110/18
12 wt	

63

PRACTICE: THREAD SAMPLER

This practice session may be short or long, depending on the size of your thread collection and how many threads you choose to stitch. This is a great exercise to do with a friend, especially if you have a limited thread collection.

DOODLE

Doodle the outline of a spool. Fill each spool with a decorative motif. Challenge yourself to create a spool in one continuous line for easier stitching.

SUPPLIES

+ 1 quick quilt sandwich (page 14)

+ Top thread (variety of threads that contrasts well with the top fabric)

+ Bobbin thread (50-weight or lighter in a color that matches the top thread)

GET READY

1. Set up your machine for quilting (see page 8). You may need to change the needle size depending on the different threads you'll be stitching.

2. Use white chalk and a ruler to draw a 6 × 6 grid, spacing the lines 3" apart, on the top fabric of the quilt sandwich. Using a permanent marker, label the first two rows "Light," the second two rows "Medium," and the last two rows "Heavy."

STITCH

When making your thread sampler, look for a variety of fibers and weights from several manufacturers.

1. Choose one thread and stitch the grid outline.

2. Stitch a simple motif in each of the squares, changing threads after every motif.

3. Use a permanent marker to label each stitched motif with the thread type, fiber, and brand.

4. Whenever you purchase a new thread, add it to your sampler.

EVALUATE

+ Do you have a variety of thread colors?

+ Do you have cotton, polyester, and rayon threads?

+ Do you have light, medium, and heavyweight threads?

+ Do you have threads with and without sheen?

+ Do you have a favorite bobbin thread?

Light　　　　　Medium　　　　　Heavy

Aurifil
Cotton　　80wt

Aurifil
Cotton　　50wt

Aurifil
Cotton　　28wt

Mirage·Wonder
Valdani　　30wt

Sulky
Polyester　　60wt
Poly-Lite

Sulky
Cotton　　50wt
Cotton+Steel

Sulky
Cotton　　30wt

Bottom Line
Polyester　　60wt
Superior

SoFine·Superior
Polyester　　50wt 3ply

King Tut·Superior
Cotton　　40wt
Superior

Microquilter
Polyester　　100wt
Superior

Magnifico
Polyester　　40wt

Sulky
Rayon　　40wt

Twister Tweed
Rayon　　35wt
Robison-Anton

LESSON 13:

BATTING BASICS

In addition to the pattern of your quilt top, three other elements work together to determine the overall look and feel of your finished quilt: thread, batting, and quilting motifs.

CREATE BATTING SAMPLES

If you haven't given much thought to batting in the past, you're about to now! Different fiber contents and lofts will affect how your quilt looks, so think about how your quilt will be used, whether or not it will be washed, and if so, do you like a crinkled or smooth finish. The best way to choose the right batting is to make samples.

In the previous lessons, you've used lightweight cotton batting to create quilt sandwiches. From now on, sample a variety of batting fibers to achieve different design goals. In this lesson, try a wool or polyester batting to compare it to the cotton samples.

Include the batting fiber brand and weight on the label of all your quilts to evaluate how they perform over time.

COMPARING BATTING TYPES

Cotton, polyester, wool, bamboo, and silk all have distinct characteristics and are the most common types of batting. Some manufacturers combine two fibers in one batting to take advantage of the best characteristics of both fibers. For example, wool/cotton batting is lightweight and more crease resistant than cotton batting and cotton/polyester batting offers more loft and less weight than cotton batting. The key to understanding how a particular batting will look and feel in your quilts is to read batting labels and to make washed and unwashed samples (fig. A).

It can be challenging to evaluate batting because local quilt shops and online stores have limited collections. Many manufacturers offer free sample boards of their complete product lines and are a great way to compare loft, fiber, and weight.

BATTING CHECKLIST

Before choosing a batting, think about how the quilt will be used and what your preferences are. For example, if you're creating a bed quilt, you may want it to be soft, warm, and easily washable. On the other hand, if you're making an art quilt, you might prefer that the quilt remains flat and not show fold lines. It's also important to check the spacing guidelines recommended by the manufacturer. Some types of batting require closer quilting than others. Make a checklist. Which of the following are most important for your design and use goals?

Do you prefer your quilts wrinkly or smooth? Many quilts become wrinkly or textured after washing. This is due to shrinkage of the batting. Choose polyester or wool batting for the least shrinkage and cotton batting if you prefer a textured appearance after washing. The photo shows the same batting and block, but the one on the top was laundered and is gently wrinkled (fig. B, page 69).

Do you like quilts that are flat or puffy? Flatness or puffiness is known as loft. Most manufacturers offer battings from low to high loft. Polyester and wool have the most loft, while cotton is usually low to medium loft.

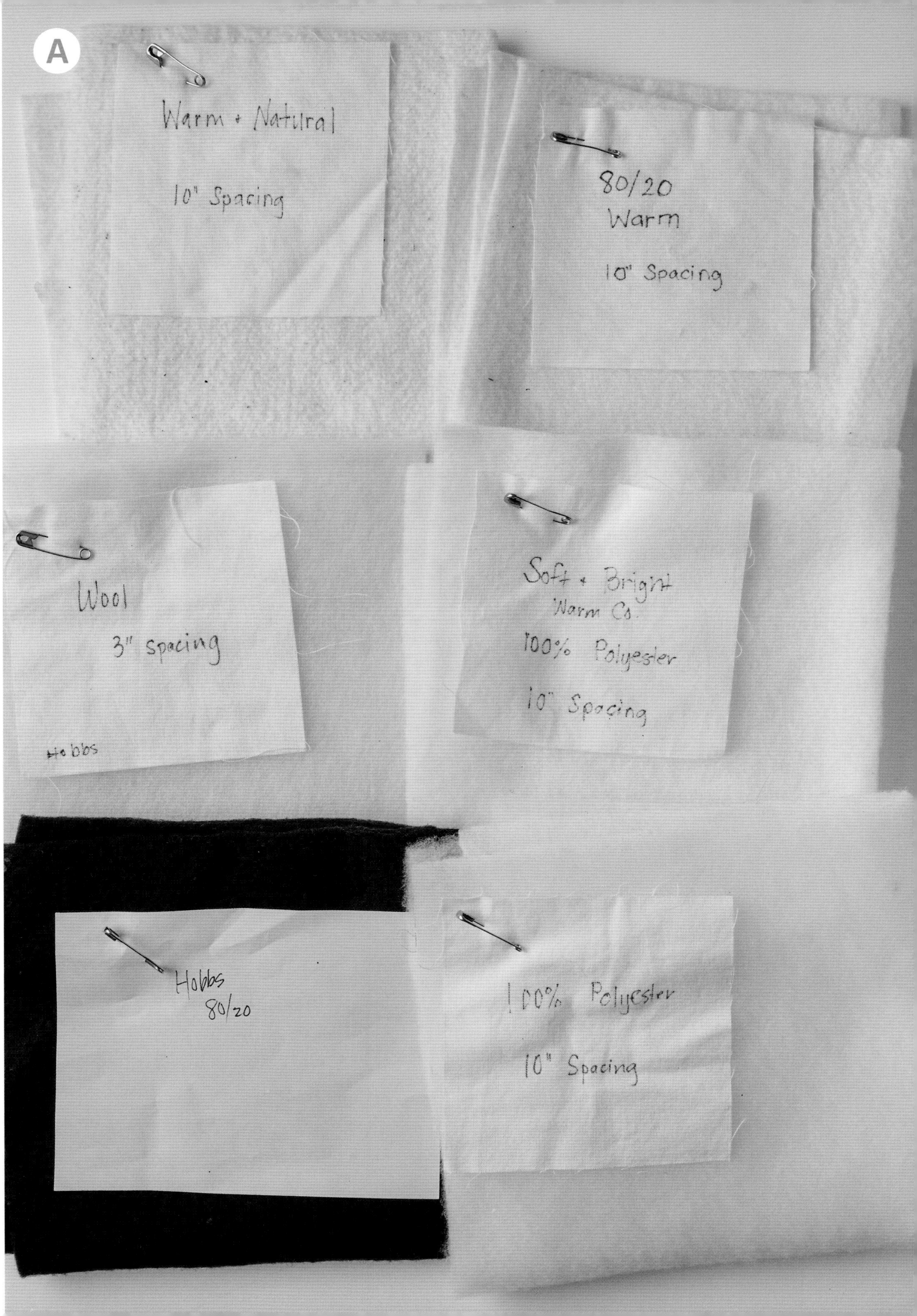

A

Warm + Natural

10" Spacing

80/20
Warm

10" Spacing

Wool

3" Spacing

Hobbs

Soft + Bright
"Warm Co.
100% Polyester

10" Spacing

Hobbs
80/20

100% Polyester

10" Spacing

Will the quilt be washed or remain unwashed? Almost all quilt batting can be washed (including wool). Some fibers (like polyester) dry more quickly than others and with less shrinkage. If the quilt will be washed, be sure to follow the manufacturer's guidelines for maximum quilt spacing.

Is it important that the quilt not show fold lines? Cotton batting tends to reveal fold lines (fig. C), whereas polyester and wool batting are more resistant to creases.

Do you want the quilt to be lightweight or heavyweight? There are lightweight and heavyweight variations of most fibers.

Are you trying to create a trapunto-like effect? Fibers with high loft create special design effects. Wool is especially nice for creating the effect of stuffed (trapunto) quilting (fig. D).

How far apart do you intend to quilt? If you stitch beyond the recommended spacing, the batting will bunch up between the stitching lines after washing. You can always stitch closer that the recommended maximum spacing. For some manufacturers' recommendations, see fig. A on page 67.

What colors are in your quilt? If your quilt has a lot of white blocks, choose a bleached or white batting to prevent the color of the batting from showing through. If your quilt contains mostly dark colors, considering using a dark batting.

Join Batting Pieces

To combine two pieces of batting, overlap the edges on top of a cutting board. Use a rotary cutter to cut a slightly wavy line through the overlapped pieces (fig E). Remove the scraps and join the two edges with hand sewing or with lightweight fusible tape.

PRACTICE: DIAGONAL SUNBURSTS

In this practice session, you'll make a quilted sample using polyester batting and different weights of thread.

DOODLE

Draw six squares in your sketchbook. Divide four of the squares in half diagonally to create half-square triangles. Divide the remaining two squares into quarters diagonally to create quarter-square triangles. Doodle a partial sun motif in each triangle by drawing a half or quarter circle with triangles around it. Try different combinations and positions for the sun motifs, filling one or all of the triangles.

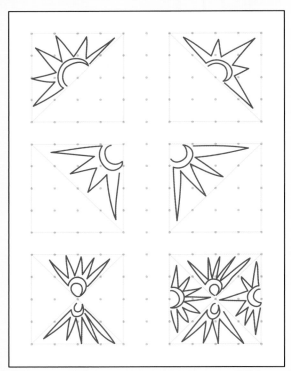

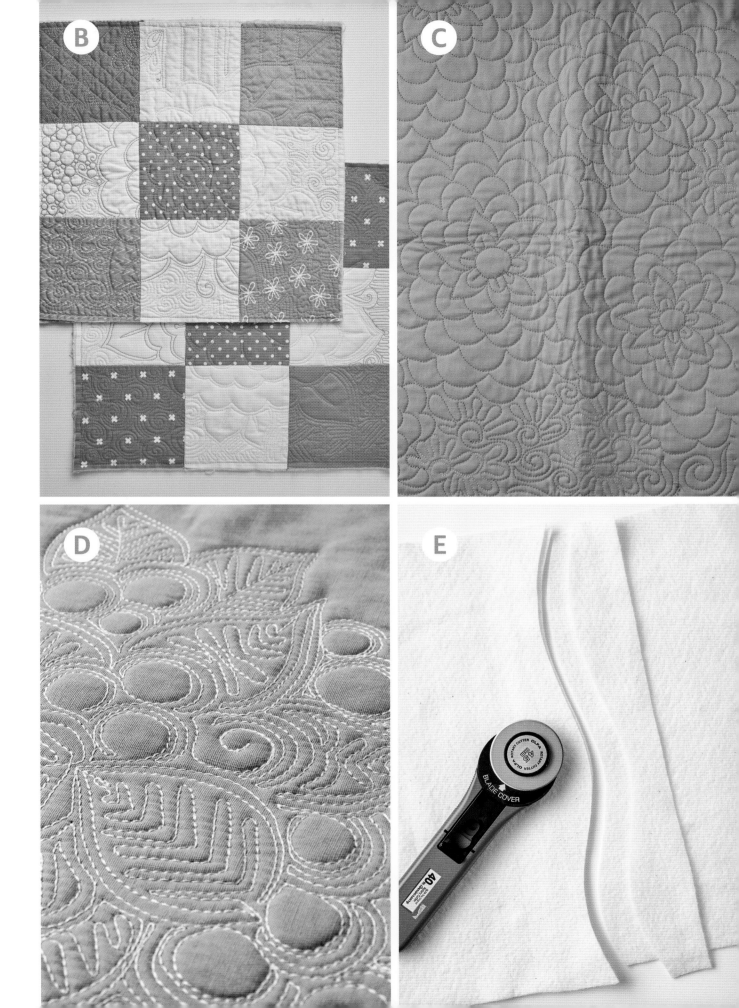

SUPPLIES

+ 1 quick quilt sandwich with light- or mediumweight polyester batting. Add pins if necessary to prevent the layers from shifting while quilting (page 90).

+ Top thread (medium or heavyweight thread that contrasts well with the top fabric and lightweight thread in a color that matches the background fabric)

+ Bobbin thread (50-weight or lighter in a color that matches the top thread)

GET READY

1. Set up your machine for quilting. (See Lesson 12: Thread Matters on page 58 to choose the correct needle size for the thread weight.)

2. Use white chalk and a ruler to mark an 8" square in the center of the top fabric on the quilt sandwich. Divide the square in half diagonally. On each side of the diagonal line, draw a line ½" from the marked line. Mark a 2½"-wide border around the center square.

STITCH

1. Stitch a slightly wavy line on all the marked lines, except the center diagonal line. Begin and end each line with a stitch-in-place knot.

2. Stitch zigzags and Messy Spirals between the border lines. As you stitch the border, stitch a Messy Spiral in the corners to change direction.

3. Change thread to a contrasting heavyweight thread. Insert the appropriate-size needle. Using your favorite doodled composition, stitch the partial sun motifs. Begin and end each line of stitching with the curlicue knot.

4. Choose a second contrasting heavyweight thread, if desired. Stitch around the border using a basic spiral and a zigzag in the corners. Stitch and echo stitch around the perimeter. For more emphasis, closely echo stitch this line of stitching. Begin and end with a curlicue knot.

5. Complete the exercise by stitching your signature and the date.

6. With a permanent marker, label the back of the quilt with the brand of batting, fiber content, and weight.

EVALUATE

+ What batting do you use most frequently?

+ What factors do you usually consider when choosing batting?

+ Do you always use the same batting or do you choose the batting to suit the project?

+ How does polyester batting compare to the cotton batting used in previous lessons?

+ Did the batting seem to make a difference in the machine tension settings?

LESSON 14:

QUILT MARKING

Marking tools abound because a single perfect marking device does not exist! It's important to choose the right marking tool for any quilt. Light and dark fabrics require separate tools and marking on printed fabric can be challenging. While a marked line must be easy to see, it's equally important that it's easy to remove. If your project won't be washed, choose a marking tool that is easy to brush off or is air erasable. Create test samples to compare marking pens and find your favorite.

THE BEST TOOL FOR THE JOB

Look for marking tools that are:

Easy to see. While free-motion quilting, you need to clearly see markings under the sewing machine in order to maintain a smooth stitching line. Even a slight hesitation leads to uneven stitches. Avoid tools that smudge easily.

Easy to remove. Many quilters have been disappointed to find their quilts diminished by marks that don't come out. Some marks can be removed by wiping with a microfiber cloth, others come out with steaming or pressing, while still others require washing, are air erasable, or require special techniques, depending on the tool. So, consider how you'll care for the final piece before choosing marking tools. For projects that won't be washed, choose marking tools that are air erasable or come off easily with wiping and don't require washing.

Reliable. Dried-out markers and broken pencils make quilting frustrating. Toss out ineffective tools and look for ones that are dependable.

TEST!

Test all marking tools on *all* the fabrics you've used in your quilt *before* using the marking tools on the quilt. Determine the best method for removing the marks and be sure to test the effects of heat. Some marking tools are set by heat and others are removed with heat. Every time you add a marking tool to your collection, test it to determine its best uses and the best way to remove it.

MY FAVORITE MARKERS

The following are my favorite marking tools.

White chalk. It's easy to see on medium to dark fabrics and brushes off easily—no washing required. When using chalk, mark the quilt after it's layered with batting and backing to prevent the lines from smudging. Chalk comes in many forms. Below are my two favorite chalk markers.

+ The Dritz chalk cartridge is a convenient chalk holder, allowing you to hold chalk like a pencil. The chalk set contains a sharpener and several colors of chalk. Save the colors for other purposes. Use only white chalk. If you need to use other colors, test carefully!

+ The Clover Chaco Liner is an easy way to mark straight lines. It rolls quickly against the edge of a ruler and through straight-line stencils.

Crayola Ultra-Clean washable markers. These inexpensive markers are designed to be removable from most surfaces, including fabric. They come in a package of colors that are vibrant and easy to see and that wash out easily. They're excellent for marking light-colored fabrics on projects that will be washed.

Air-erasable markers. Great for light-colored fabrics, especially when you don't want to wash the project. Markings generally disappear within hours or days so these are best for marking as you go.

Painter's tape. Painter's tape is a low-tack tape that makes marking straight lines easy. Stitch next to the tape and reposition it several times before replacing each piece of tape.

WHEN TO MARK

Some quilters like to mark the entire quilt before beginning to quilt; others mark as they go. If you mark before layering the quilt, choose a marking tool that won't brush off or smudge while layering and moving the quilt.

PRACTICE: TESTING MARKERS

In this practice session, you'll try different markers to determine your favorites.

GET READY

1. If you already have a collection of marking pens, pencils, and markers, collect them all in one place. Toss out any broken pencils or dried-out markers.

2. Use three pieces of fabric to test each marker: a light solid, a dark solid, and a print fabric. With a permanent marker, mark one side of each fabric "Pressed" and the other side "Not Pressed."

MARK AND ASSESS

1. Mark each of the sections with every marking tool. As you're marking, consider:
   + How wide or thin is the line? How visible is it?
   + Which marking tool is most visible on dark fabric, light fabric, or printed fabric?
   + Does the pencil break easily or the marker dry out quickly?

2. Wipe the marks with a microfiber or other cloth.
   + Is the mark easy to remove by wiping?
   + Does the mark smudge?

3. Iron the sections marked "Pressed."
   + Is the marked line erased with heat?
   + Does the mark change color from the heat?

4. Rinse the swatches under cold water.
   + Which marks rinse off easily?
   + Which marks remain bold?
   + Did pressing with heat make a difference?

5. Begin a collection of your favorite marking tools.

STITCH

If you have extra time, create a quick fat-quarter quilt sandwich. Choose your favorite marking tool to draw a 2" grid. Spend 20 minutes filling in the grid with your doodles. Relax and have fun. The grid will make your random doodle stitching look like a composition!

EVALUATE

+ Which are your favorite marking tools?
+ Do you have a marker for light fabrics?
+ Do you have a tool for marking dark fabrics?
+ Do you have any tools that are frustrating to use? Why?

Press   Not Pressed

chalk   chalk

crayola   crayola

Pressed   Not Pressed

Pressed   Not Pressed

Clover blue pen   clover blue
                             pen
Crayola   crayola
Crayola   crayola

LESSON 15:

DIVIDE AND CONQUER DESIGN

Every quilt seems huge when you're trying to plan how to quilt it. Divide and conquer! Use tape, rulers, and stencils to divide the quilt into sections that are easier to design and more manageable to quilt. Or start with a motif and divide the quilt into sections to accommodate the motif.

SUBDIVIDING FOR DESIGN

When you're not sure how to quilt an area, try subdividing it into smaller parts. For example, divide a long, wide border into squares. Then look for a motif to fill each square. You'll focus on quilting only one square at a time. Use seamlines as guidelines whenever possible to minimize marking. Use yardsticks and rulers to split large areas of negative space into smaller shapes. Once you have a broad outline, choosing motifs and arranging designs is easier.

Yardsticks. Use a yardstick or long, straight ruler to create long horizontal, vertical, or diagonal lines across the quilt to create major divisions. Mark the lines with a chalk wheel or tape, then use the lines to align stencils, smaller rulers, or motifs.

Rulers. Rotary-cutting rulers are available in a variety of shapes and sizes and are handy when designing a large quilt. Partition large sections of the quilt with rulers from your collection. Place square rulers on a horizontal axes or rotate them to create different design effects. Use diamond, half-circle, and hexagon rulers, plus your entire collection of cutting rulers, to create interesting subdivisions for quilting.

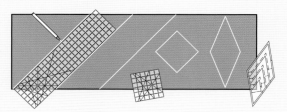

FINDING THE CENTER

Finding the center of a quilt block is often helpful when positioning a design element. The quickest way to find the center of a square or rectangle is to draw diagonal lines from one corner to the opposite corner in both directions. The intersection of the two lines is the center of the shape. Use the center point to place large motifs within a block. Or use the diagonal lines to divide the block into triangles. Look for motifs to fill each triangle, or place motifs along the diagonal lines.

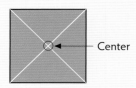

DIVIDING IN HALF OR QUARTERS

After drawing diagonal lines to find the center, use a ruler to mark the horizontal and vertical center lines, dividing the area into squares or rectangles. Look for motifs to fill these shapes.

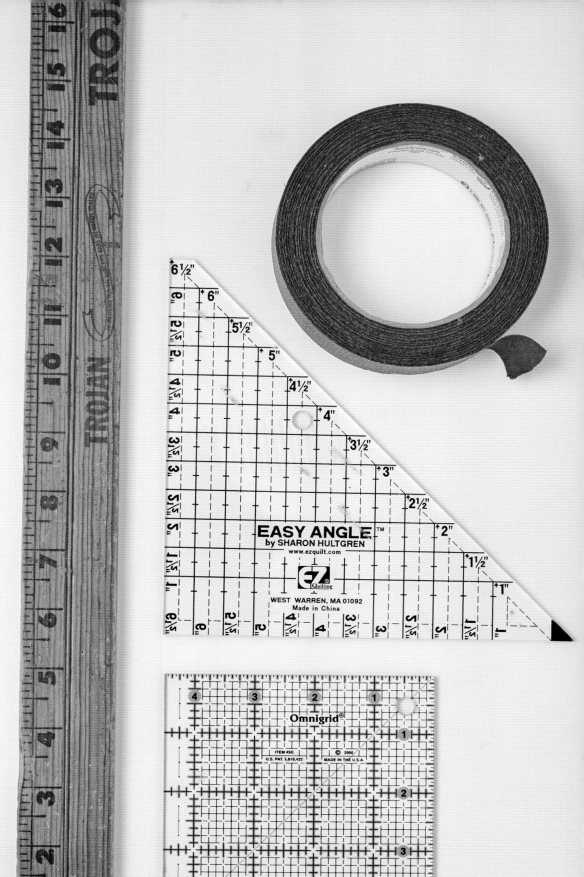

To divide a large rectangle into smaller sections, start by drawing a small square in the center. Then use a yardstick or long ruler to extend the marked lines.

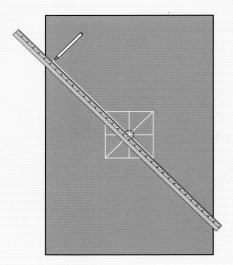

PRACTICE: PIANO KEY BORDER

In this practice session, you'll divide the quilting space to make design and stitching more manageable.

DOODLE

In your sketchbook, draw several squares and rectangles. Find the center of the squares and divide the squares in half diagonally. Divide the squares into quarters. Repeat with the rectangles. Doodle a variety of motifs within each section. Try partial motifs like suns and flowers or background fill motifs. Or use one of the four favorite motifs, page 38.

SUPPLIES

+ 1 quick quilt sandwich with wool or medium-loft polyester batting (page 14)

+ Top thread (heavyweight thread that contrasts well with the top fabric)

+ Bobbin thread (50-weight or lighter in a color that matches the top thread)

GET READY

1. Set up your machine for quilting (see page 8).

2. Use white chalk and a ruler to mark a 12" square in the center of the quilt top. Add a 2"-wide border around the center square. Mark diagonal lines to find the square's center point. Then mark vertical and horizontal lines to divide the design into quarters. Start at the center mark on each border and mark a line ½" from each side of the center mark. Mark lines spaced 1" apart in each border.

STITCH

1. Stitch a slightly wavy line around the center square. Echo stitch the line and knot off.

2. As you stitch the outer line, stop at each marked line. Stitch along the drawn line, move over one or two stitches, and stitch back to the outer line. Continue to stitch the entire border in this way to create a modified piano key border.

3. Echo stitch the outer border and knot off.

4. Save the sample for Lesson 16: Negative Space Designs (page 80).

EVALUATE

+ Look at your current quilts. Would subdividing the blocks simplify the design?

+ Do you have a collection of rulers in an assortment of shapes and sizes you could use to subdivide a quilt?

+ Is there anything else around the house, such as plates, coasters, or DVDs, that you could use to create interesting shapes within your quilt?

LESSON 16:

NEGATIVE SPACE DESIGNS

Tracing around a template is a great way to define a shape on your quilt top. Templates are easy to make and use. Trace the template, then add dense quilting around the shape to create a negative space design.

CREATING NEGATIVE SPACE

The negative space, or unquilted area, is more visible than heavily quilted areas. Use theme-related shapes (fig. A) to add complexity to a design, or use simple shapes to add texture to the quilt.

The fish shape on the left (fig. B) is outline stitched, echo stitched, and then surrounded with dense stitching to create more definition. The fish on the right isn't outlined; instead, dense stitching alone creates the fish shape's outline. The denser the quilting, the more the negative shape will pop.

Batting Matters

High-loft batting will make negative space even more noticeable. Use wool or polyester batting to create a trapunto-like quilt design, such as the quilted star shown here.

PRACTICE: FISH QUILT

In this practice session, you'll make a template and add dense stitching around a shape to create a negative-space design.

SUPPLIES

+ Quick quilt sandwich from Lesson 15: Divide and Conquer Design (page 76)
+ Top thread (heavyweight thread that contrasts well with the top fabric)
+ Bobbin thread (50-weight or lighter in a color that matches the top thread)
+ Heavy cardboard or cereal box
+ Lightweight paper
+ Glue stick
+ White chalk or Crayola Ultra-Clean marker

MAKE A TEMPLATE

Use the patter on page 82 to draw a simple fish or other motif onto lightweight paper. Roughly cut out the shape and glue it onto cardboard. Cut out the template directly on the line.

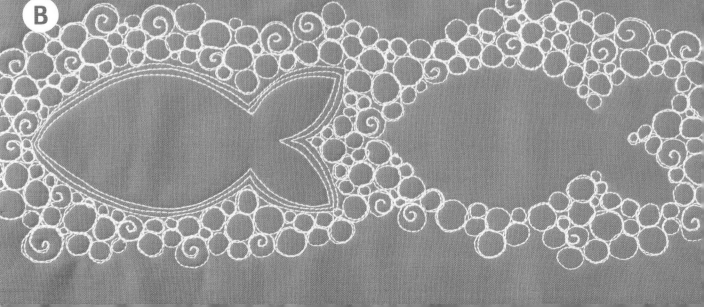

DOODLE

Use a pencil to trace the fish shape into your sketchbook. Doodle around the shape with a darker pen. Erase the shape's outline to reveal a negative-space design.

GET READY

1. Position the template in the center of the quilt sandwich from Lesson 15: Divide and Conquer Design (page 76) which has been divided into eight sections.

2. Use your favorite marking tool to outline the template. (See Lesson 14: Quilt Marking on page 72.)

3. Set up your machine for quilting (see page 8).

STITCH

1. Stitch around the fish shape and closely echo stitch the line for more design impact.

2. Stitch different motifs in each of the eight sections, alternate two motifs, or add any variety of background fill motifs to complete the quilt.

3. Complete the exercise by stitching your signature and the date.

EVALUATE

+ Looking at your doodles, do you have a shape that you repeat frequently? Could you turn that shape into a template?

+ Review your quilts. What shapes are repeated within the quilt tops? Could you use an appliqué shape to create a machine-quilting template?

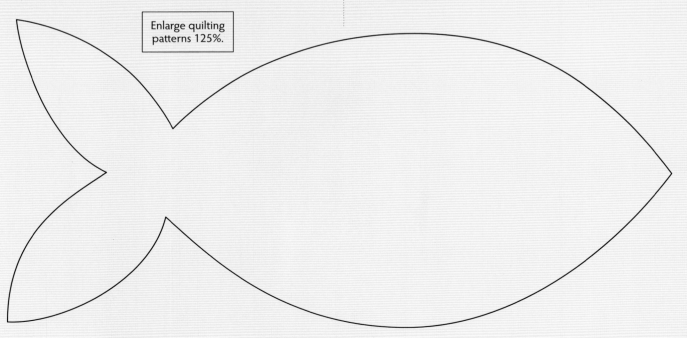

Enlarge quilting patterns 125%.

82

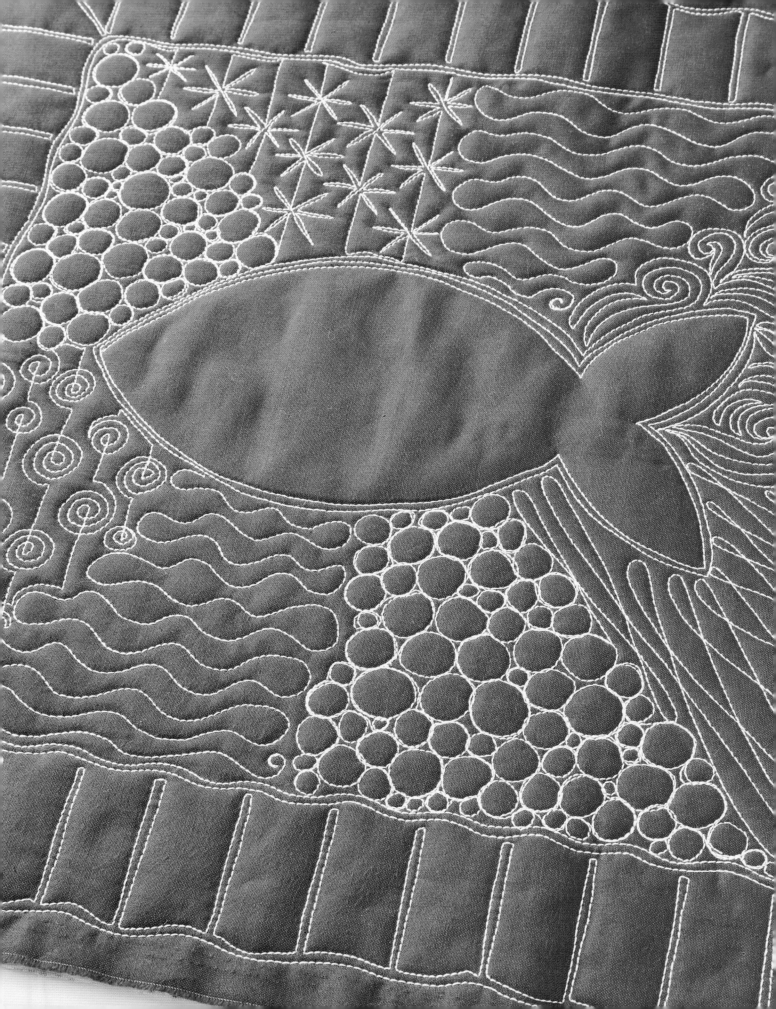

LESSON 17:
DESIGNING WITH STENCILS

Once a quilt is divided into smaller sections, stencils are a great tool for adding decorative elements or creating placement lines for motifs. You can choose from hundreds of stencils in an assortment of styles and patterns to help personalize quilts.

STENCILS

Two types of stencils are used for machine-quilting design. First, grid stencils help you keep quilting lines straight—or you can stitch on the lines to create a variety of textures. Second, decorative or theme-related stencils add interesting motifs and patterns.

Grids. Grids and line stencils are invaluable for accurate placement of quilting lines (fig. A, page 87). Stitch on the gridded lines to create texture or use the grid to create even spacing for other motifs. For example, you can stitch on the lines of a 2" grid or use the grid lines to evenly space spirals. Grid stencils are available in standard squares as well as diamonds, circles, and other shapes. Turn a 1" grid into a larger grid simply by marking every other line.

Decorative. Decorative stencils designed for machine quilting are often labeled "continuous-line designs," meaning you can stitch the entire motif without stopping and starting a new line of stitching. Other decorative stencils require multiple lines of stitching, crossing over previous lines of stitching or stopping points, which requires knotting off.

TIPS FOR USING STENCILS

Here are a few tips to keep in mind when picking out and using a quilting stencil.

Choose stencils that are simple, but not too simple! Look for designs that are too difficult to learn by doodling. It's easier to doodle and develop the muscle memory to quilt a wavy line than to mark a wavy line, stitch it, and then remove the markings. It will always save time if you can learn to quilt a motif without marking.

Be sure the stencil isn't too complicated. Before you pick a stencil, see if you can trace a line with your finger to determine a path to travel. Some stencils are beautiful but complicated and not fun to quilt—especially when your quilt is squished under the harp space and you can't see the full design.

Choose the right size. Stencil designs are usually offered in a range of sizes. Choose the size that fits the dimensions of your quilt or subdivide the shape to accommodate the stencil.

Remember corners. When selecting a border stencil, you may also need to purchase the matching corner stencil to create a continuous design. In fig. B on page 87, the corner stencil is taped to the border stencil to make the curve.

Test before marking. Before marking the stencil lines on the quilt, test the design on a practice block or border. Be sure you understand the stitching order and check the fit before marking the entire quilt. Use the stencil's registration marks to be sure the design is aligned properly.

Mark the entire line. After marking the stencil on the quilt, go back and fill in the gaps in the line that the stencil leaves out. When the quilt is under the needle, it's easier to follow an unbroken line. In fig. C, the bird's nest on the left shows the traced stencil, while the one on the right shows all the connected lines for easier quilting.

Use a pounce pads. Pounce pads, shown on page 85, are a fast way to mark stencil lines. They contain loose, powdered chalk which can be swiped over the stencil to mark the line. To prevent smudging, spray lightly with hair spray after marking. To remove the line, the chalk is ironed or brushed off. If you added hair spray, wash the quilt to remove the marks and residue. (As always, be sure to follow manufacturer's instructions and test first on a scrap of your quilt fabric!)

PRACTICE: ORANGE PEEL DESIGN

In this practice session, you'll use a grid stencil to create an Orange Peel quilting design.

DOODLE

Use a ruler or grid stencil to draw a 1" grid in your sketchbook. Doodle a wavy line along one vertical line on the marked grid, moving from one side of the line to the other. On the same line, doodle in the opposite direction to create an Orange Peel design. As you have time, play with stencils and templates to create a variety of designs.

SUPPLIES

+ 1 quick quilt sandwich (page 14)
+ Top thread (heavyweight thread that contrasts well with the top fabric)

+ Bobbin thread (50-weight or lighter in a color that matches the top thread)
+ 1" grid quilting stencil (optional; see "Supplies and Tools" on page 10)
+ Clover Chaco Liner

GET READY

1. Set up your machine for quilting (see page 8).

2. Use white chalk and a ruler to mark an 8" square in the center of the top fabric on the quilt sandwich.

3. Use a 1" grid stencil to mark a grid in the center of the square. If you don't have a stencil, use chalk and a straight ruler to make a 1" grid in the square. Try the Clover chalk wheel for quick, straight lines when using either a stencil or ruler.

STITCH

1. Starting at the bottom left, stitch a wavy line along a vertical line on the marked grid, curving from one side of the line to the other at the line intersections.

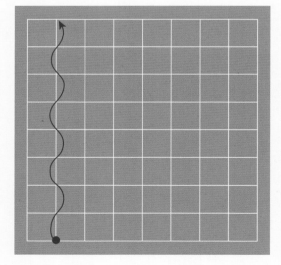

Start.

2. Stitch back down the same line, in the opposite direction, again curving from one side of the marked line to the other. Stitch a curved line along the bottom to the next vertical line. Starting at the bottom of the next vertical line, stitch a wavy line to the top of the grid.

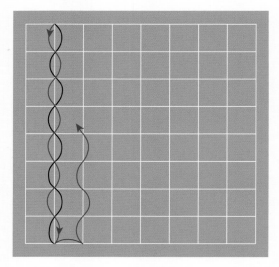

3. Continue stitching wavy lines to complete all the vertical rows.

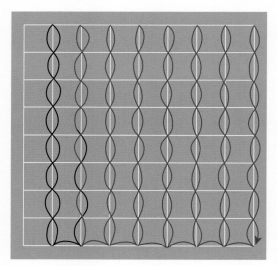

4. Repeat to stitch the marked horizontal lines in the same way. Travel to the horizontal lines by carefully stitching over the last wave in the line. Then stitch the rows from right to left and back again. Review Lesson 10: Directional Stitching (page 48) and rotate the quilt, if desired.

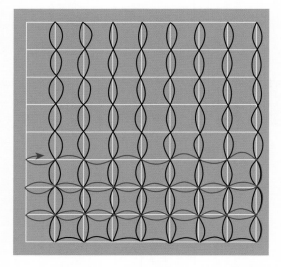

5. Set the sample aside for the Lesson 20: Travel Stitching (page 100).

EVALUATE

+ Were you able to see the marked line easily while stitching?

+ Do you find it easier to follow a marked line or to free-motion quilt a memorized motif?

+ Could you use a part of the grid stencil to create a different design?

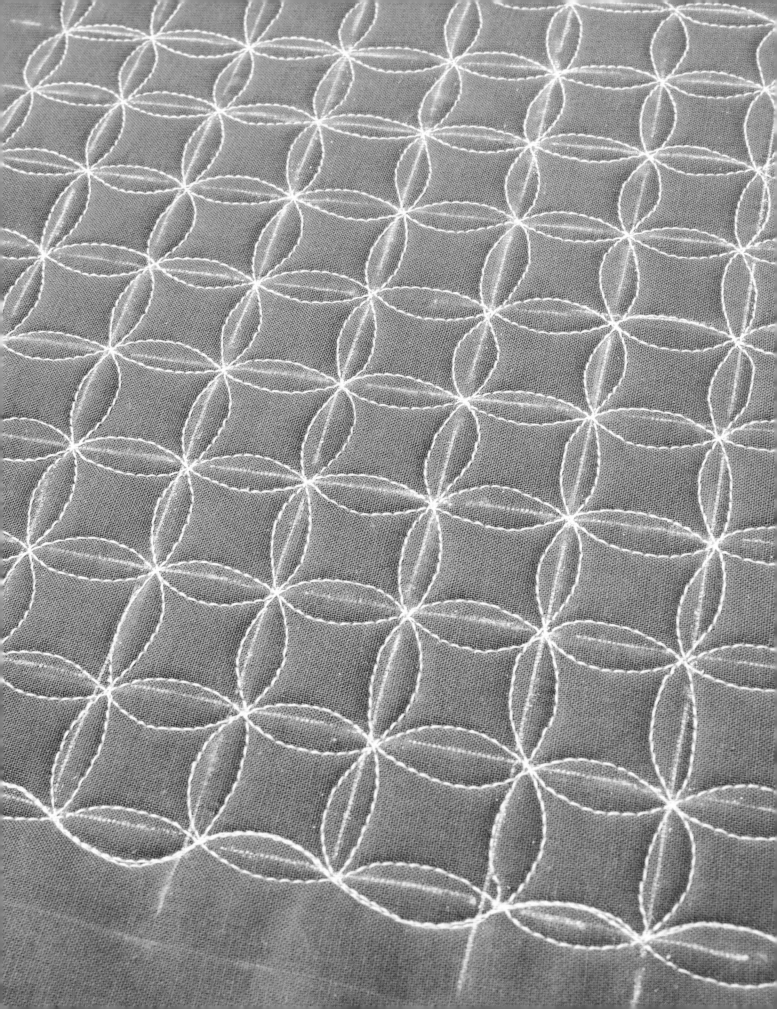

BASTING WITH PINS AND SPRAY

All quilts require basting to keep the three layers of the quilt from shifting during the machine-quilting process. Pressing the layers together with a steam iron works for basting very small quilts with cotton batting. For larger quilts, pin basting and spray basting are best. Leave thread basting for hand-quilting projects; long basting threads will get caught in the machine quilting and are difficult to remove.

PIN BASTING

The easiest way to pin baste a large quilt is to use a large table or countertop. Use leg extenders to elevate the table to a more comfortable height.

SUPPLIES

In addition to a quilt top, batting, backing, and a large table, you'll need the following supplies for pin basting (fig. A).

+ Painter's tape
+ Coin or button
+ Large binder clips
+ Machine-quilting gloves
+ Size 2 safety pins
+ Kwik clip or spoon

PREPARE THE LAYERS

1. Remove the batting from the package and allow the fibers to relax for at least 24 hours before layering the quilt. Trim the batting at least 4" to 8" larger than the top. Fold the batting in half vertically and horizontally.

2. Carefully press the quilt top and trim any stray threads from the seam allowances. Fold the top in half vertically and horizontally, right sides together.

3. Cut or piece the quilt backing so it's 4" to 8" larger than the quilt top. Press the backing and starch (if desired). Fold the backing in half vertically and horizontally, wrong sides together. All three layers are now folded so you can find their centers (fig. B).

ASSEMBLE THE QUILT SANDWICH

1. Use painter's tape to tape a coin or button in the center of the table. That way you'll be able to find the center of the table by feel after it's covered with the backing fabric.

2. Position the folded center of the backing fabric on the table on top of the coin. Unfold the backing fabric, with the wrong side facing up. Allow the fabric to drape over the edge of the table if necessary, being careful to keep the center of the fabric along the centerline of the table.

3. Starting in the center, use binder clips or painter's tape to anchor the quilt back to the table edge. Smooth the fabric toward the edges and continue adding clips or tape until the backing is anchored to the table on all four sides and the backing is taut but not stretched (fig. C).

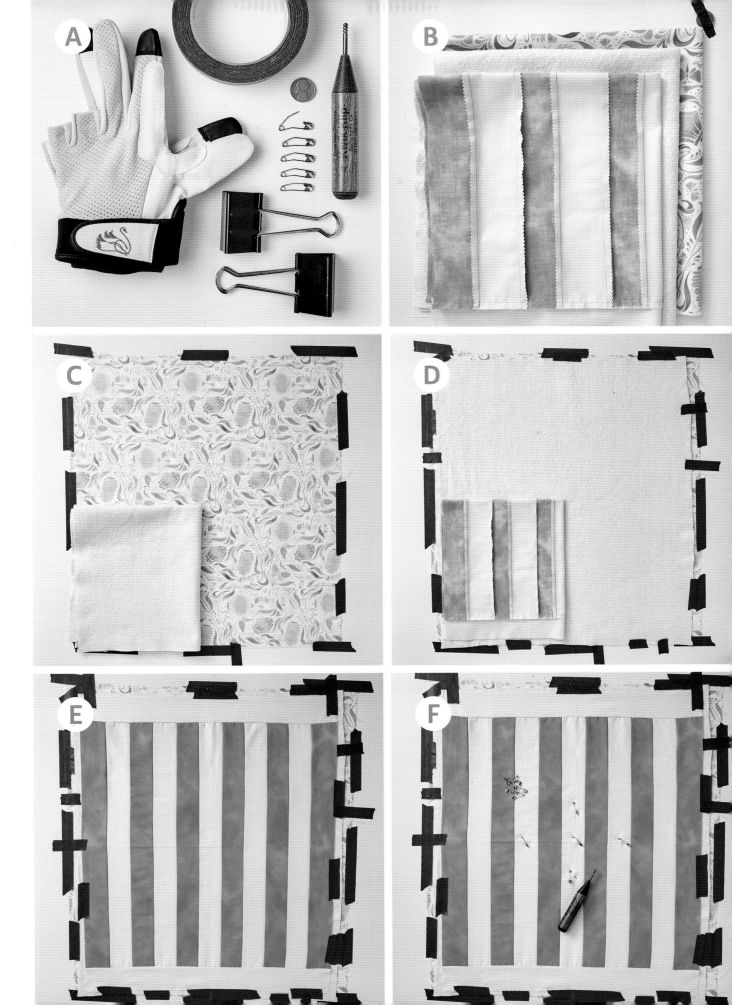

4. Center and unfold the batting on top of the backing. Working from the center, remove one binder clip at a time and reposition the clip to include the batting layer. If your backing is taped, simply add a new piece of tape to secure the batting; don't untape the backing fabric. Smooth the batting toward the edges and anchor the batting to the table along with the backing fabric (fig. D, page 91).

5. Center and unfold the quilt top over of the batting. Carefully remove each binder clip and reattach the clip to include the quilt top. If using tape, simply tape the quilt top in place, working from the center out and smoothing the quilt top as you go (fig. E, page 91). The quilt top should be taut but not stretched.

6. Starting in the center, safety pin the layers together. Space the pins 4" to 5" apart. Use the back of a spoon or a Kwik Clip to close the pins, as this will save time and wear and tear on your fingers (fig. F, page 91). Wear machine-quilting gloves to increase your grip and protect your hands.

7. After basting the center of the quilt, shift the quilt right or left and up and down on the table and repeat the process until the entire quilt is basted.

8. When the entire quilt is basted, turn the quilt over to be sure there are no folds or tucks in the backing.

SPRAY BASTING

Using basting spray is much quicker than pin basting but requires a ventilated area for spraying and a wall, floor area, or table as large as the quilt to layer the sandwich. It's helpful to have two people when positioning the layers for a large quilt. By eliminating pins, spray-basted quilts weigh less and are slightly easier to maneuver when quilting.

SUPPLIES

In addition to a quilt top, batting, backing, and a large table or floor, you'll need the following supplies for spray basting.

+ Painter's tape
+ Temporary adhesive spray (such as 505 Spray and Fix)

Spray-Basting Caution

Beware of overspray if working on carpet; it can leave a sticky residue that will attract dirt. To avoid this, lay a large bedsheet on the carpet first for protection. When you're done basting, it is easy to pop the sheet into the laundry to remove any overspray. Also, do not use basting spray if you have birds or other small pets in the house, as the chemicals can be harmful to them.

ASSEMBLE THE QUILT SANDWICH

1. Refer to "Prepare the Layers" on page 90 to prepare the quilt top, batting, and backing.

2. In a well-ventilated room or outdoors, lay the quilt top wrong side up on the floor or on a table. Following the manufacturer's recommendations, spray the wrong side of the quilt top. The fabric should feel tacky. Set the quilt top aside. You can fold the quilt top, tacky sides together, while you spray the backing.

3. Lay out the backing fabric, wrong side up, and spray it until it's tacky.

4. Place the backing wrong side up on a large floor, wall, or table (or tables) that will accommodate the entire quilt. Use painter's tape to anchor the backing in place, making sure it's taut.

5. Center the batting on top of the backing and gently smooth in place, starting in the center and working outwards. Use a long ruler to help smooth out the batting, as needed.

6. Center the prepared quilt top right side up on top of the batting and gently smooth in place, starting in the center and working outwards. Again, use a long ruler to help smooth out the batting.

7. Using the cotton setting, press the entire quilt from the back and then again on the front.

8. When the quilt is complete, wash it to remove the spray adhesive.

PRACTICE: BASTING QUILT SANDWICHES

In this practice session, we'll create a few quilt sandwiches to have on hand for practice and future lessons. For small quilt sandwiches, try spray basting on a wall. Remember to cover the surface with a sheet first before spray basting.

SUPPLIES

+ 6 fat quarters of solid fabric for tops
+ 6 fat quarters of coordinating print for backings
+ 6 pieces of any type of batting, 18" × 21"
+ Pin-basting supplies
+ Spray-basting supplies

MAKE BASTED QUILT SANDWICHES

1. Referring to "Pin Basting" on page 90, make three quilt sandwiches measuring 18" × 21".

2. Referring to "Spray Basting" on page 92, make three quilt sandwiches measuring 18" × 21".

EVALUATE

+ Which method of basting do you prefer?
+ Where do you usually baste your quilts?
+ Is there a big wall or table in your house for basting?
+ Is basting ever a limiting factor in finishing your quilts?
+ Could you use tables at a local quilt shop or library for basting large quilts?

STABILIZING AND STITCHING IN THE DITCH

Stabilizing is intended to be an invisible or semi-invisible line of stitching that prevents shifting of the layers and distortion of the quilt. Stabilizing helps outline blocks within the quilt and provides an infrastructure for all other quilting. One of the major advantages to stabilizing is it allows you to quilt any part of the quilt at any time. In quilts that are not stabilized, it's more important to quilt starting from the center, smoothing toward the edges to ease the layers together.

TWO WAYS TO STABILIZE

Stabilizing can be done by stitching in the ditch of the seamlines or by stitching a wavy line over the seamlines. Use a machine-guided technique (feed dogs engaged) to stitch in the ditch or use free-motion quilting (feed dogs disengaged) to stitch a wavy line over the seamlines. By using lightweight thread in a color that blends with the quilt, these lines will be almost invisible in the final project. The sample in fig. A is a Log Cabin mini-quilt that's been quilted in the ditch (the seamlines). The sample in fig. B shows wavy line quilting stabilizing the mini-quilt.

HOW TO STABILIZE

1. Starting in the top center of the quilt sandwich, stitch along a seamline from the top to the bottom of the quilt and knot off. Return to the top of the quilt and stitch the next long seamline to the right of center. Continue stitching all of the seamlines on the right side of the quilt until you reach the outer edge of the quilt.

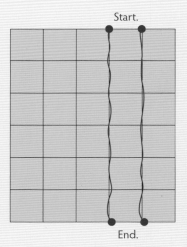

Start.

End.

2. Rotate the quilt 180° so what was the bottom edge is now at the top. Stitch from the top to the bottom along all of the remaining vertical lines of the quilt.

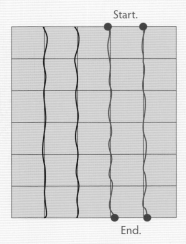

Start.

End.

3. Once all the vertical lines are stitched, rotate the quilt 90° to stitch the horizontal seamlines. Repeat step 1 and 2, stitching from the center to the outer edges and from top to bottom.

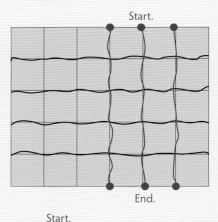

Start.

End.

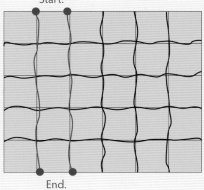

Start.

End.

QUILT TYPES

It's easy to determine where to stabilize quilts that are set in straight grids. It's more challenging for medallion quilts or quilts that are set on point. For on-point quilts, follow the seamlines in a zigzag line as shown below to create the stabilizing lines. For medallion quilts, stitch along the borders, avoiding the center medallion where the stitching lines will not be hidden by a seamline. Consider what you're trying to achieve (basic infrastructure and the ability to quilt in any order) and stabilize where you can. Baste well in areas where it would adversely affect the design to add stabilizing.

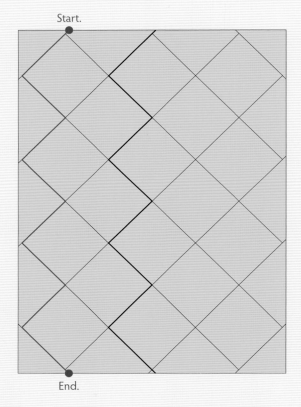

Start.

End.

STABILIZING TAKES TIME

Stabilizing has many worthwhile benefits, but it's somewhat time consuming. Use the time to get more familiar with your quilt and how it feels under the needle. While you're stabilizing, think about how you will design each section of the quilt and choose possible motifs.

96

ADDING MOTIFS AFTER STITCHING IN THE DITCH

Stitching in the ditch is simply stitching in the seamline of a block or border and is a great way to stabilize an entire quilt or to outline a block. Stitching in the ditch is used alone to complete a block, or you can add another layer of machine quilting over the block to create a different effect. Take a look at fig. C, above, which is quilted with a Flower Power motif. Did you notice the quilting in the ditch too?

Where to Begin?

Some quilters like to begin machine quilting at the center of the quilt and work outward. The idea is that the center of the quilt is the hardest, so once you finish that, the rest is easy. In addition, you can smooth the layers toward the edges as you quilt. I recommend stabilizing the quilt, which allows you to begin quilting wherever you feel comfortable. Then you can tackle the challenging middle of the quilt in short sessions. As you proceed and remove pins, the quilt gets less bulky, making the quilt lighter, and stitching the more challenging areas is a little less difficult.

LESSON 19: STABILIZING AND STITCHING IN THE DITCH

PRACTICE: OUTLINE AND ALLOVER QUILTING

In this practice session, you'll first stitch a block in the ditch before adding an allover motif.

DOODLE

In your notebook, practice doodling allover motifs like Flower Power (page 40) and Starry Night, as shown below.

SUPPLIES

+ Prepare a pieced quilt sandwich referring to "Quilt Sandwich Option," above right.

+ Top thread (lightweight thread for stabilizing and mediumweight thread for allover motifs)

+ Bobbin thread (50-weight or lighter in a color that matches the top thread)

GET READY

Set up your machine for machine-guided quilting with a walking foot or even-feed mechanism (see page 8) and lightweight thread.

Quilt Sandwich Option

Cut 36 squares, 2½" × 2½", from a variety of prints and solids. Piece them together to make a 12" × 12" checkerboard block. Add a 1¼"-wide inner border and a 2"-wide outer border. Using any batting you wish, layer the quilt top, batting, and backing. Spray or pin baste. Or, if you want to get straight to quilting, use white chalk and a ruler to draw a 6 × 6 grid, spacing the lines 1" apart, on the top fabric of the quilt sandwich. Draw a ¾"-wide border around the center square. Add a 1½"-wide outer border.

STITCH

1. Stitch in the ditch, starting on the top of the middle seam or marked line to stabilize the quilt sandwich. Knot off. Stitch the next seamline to the right. Rotate the quilt 180° and stitch the remaining vertical seams. Stitch the horizontal seams or marked lines, starting in the center and knotting off in between each row.

2. Switch your machine to a free-motion quilting set up. With mediumweight thread, stitch the allover motif to cover the quilt top.

EVALUATE

+ How do you like the look of stitch-in-the-ditch quilting?

+ How long did it take you to stabilize the quilt?

+ If you stitched in the ditch, did you find areas where it was difficult to stay in the ditch?

TRAVEL STITCHING

"Traveling" or "travel stitching" refers to the quilting lines needed to move from one motif to another or from one block to another, rather than knotting off and cutting the thread. Some motifs are designed to transition from one motif to another as part of the design; other motifs require some type of travel stitching.

TRAVELING

Whenever you're free-motion quilting, you may find your stitching line comes to a dead end without a clear path to travel to the next motif. You have several options (six to be exact!) for traveling to the next line to be stitched. The type of traveling you choose depends on the motif, block, and the thread. Travel stitching isn't just for airplanes (fig. A)!

RETRACE

You can often stitch over another line of quilting to travel to the new area. If you're using lightweight thread, the overstitched line will be barely noticeable. However, heavyweight thread can create a focal point when overstitching or retracing. Try to make the double line part of the motif. For example, double stitch the center vein of a leaf rather than the outer edge (fig. B). If the overstitching creates an unwanted focal point, choose one of the other travel schemes or knot off.

STITCH IN THE DITCH

Whether you're using lightweight or heavyweight thread, you may be able to hide the travel stitches by stitching in the ditch of a seamline, as with the mice in fig. C.

STEP OFF THE EDGE

If you're stitching near the edge of the quilt and there is a margin that will be cut off later, consider traveling in the margin (fig. D).

ADD A LOOPY LINE

Stitch a loopy line to travel from one focal motif to another, such as the loops in my umbrella quilting (fig. E). Or stitch a zigzag or other simple line to complement the focal motif or the quilt,

ECHO STITCH

Echo stitching is often the best way to travel to an open area for quilting. Follow the previous line of stitching with echo stitching to begin a new motif as I did with my cluster of leaves (fig. F).

KNOT OFF

While knotting off is the most time consuming way to travel, it may be the best choice for the design. If your stitching line cannot be hidden and it interferes with your design, then knotting may be the answer.

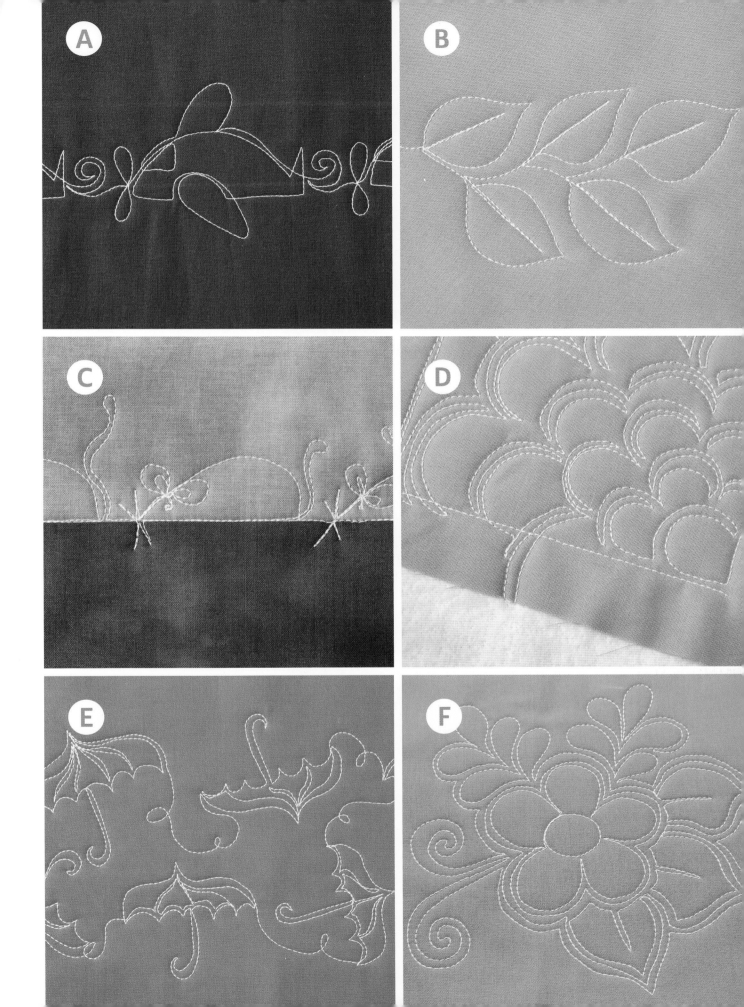

PRACTICE: FLOWER POWER AND ORANGE PEEL MEDALLION QUILT

In this practice session, you'll practice travel stitching between motifs.

DOODLE

Draw several 5" × 8" rectangles in your sketchbook. Fill each rectangle with the Flower Power motif. Try to fill the rectangle without lifting your pen, using the echoing technique to travel.

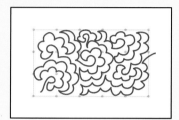

SUPPLIES

✦ Quilt sandwich from Lesson 17: Designing with Stencils (page 84)

✦ Top thread (heavyweight thread that contrasts well with the top fabric)

✦ Bobbin thread (50-weight or lighter in a color that matches the top thread)

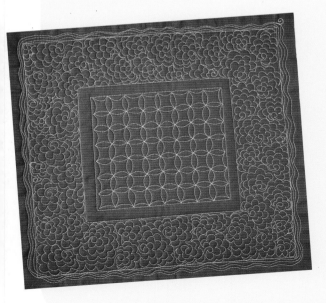

GET READY

1. On the quilt sandwich from lesson 17 where you stitched an Orange Peel design, draw a ¾"-wide border around the center square. Then draw a 5"-wide border around the middle square.

2. Set up your machine for machine-guided quilting (page 8).

STITCH

1. Stitch a straight line on the marked lines for the center, middle, and outer squares.

2. Switch your machine set up for free-motion quilting. Echo stitch slightly wavy lines around the outer marked line.

3. Fill the 5"-wide border with a background fill motif like Flower Power. When you get stuck in a corner, echo stitch the flower and continue, or knot off and begin a new line of stitching.

EVALUATE

✦ Did you get stuck in any quilting dead ends?

✦ Were you able to continue stitching without knotting off?

✦ Consider how to travel between the straight border lines. Is it best to knot off, as I did in this sample, or is there a way to travel between the rows while maintaining your design goals?

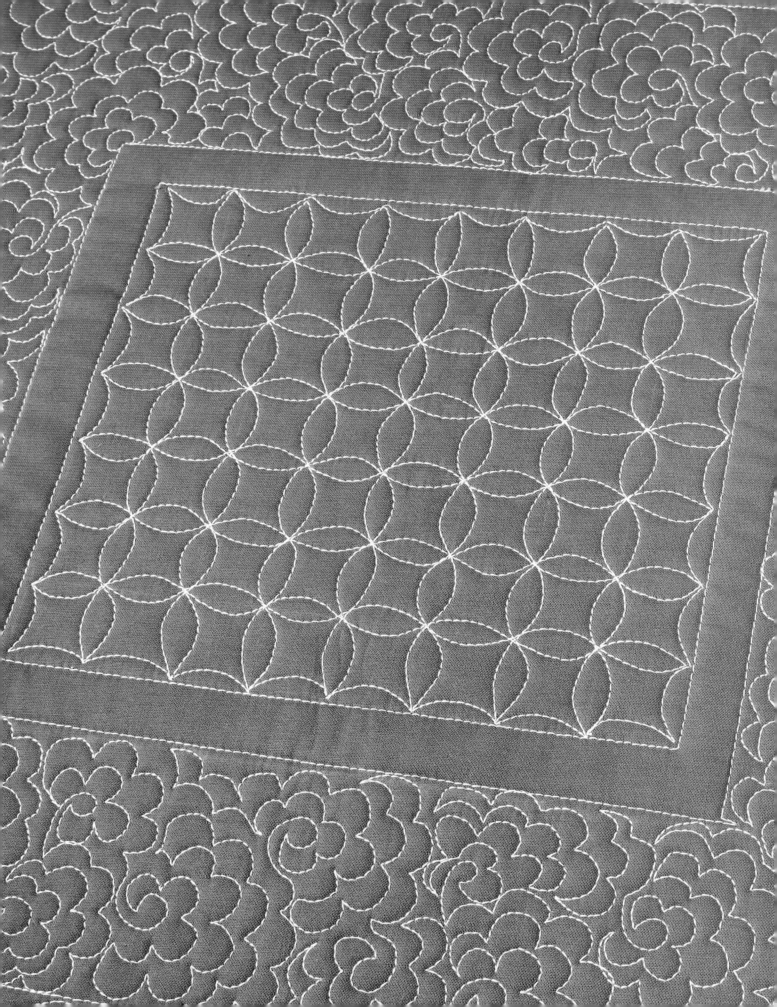

LESSON 21:

OUTLINING BASIC SHAPES

Quilting motifs stitched on pieced blocks or patterned fabrics are difficult to see, even if you use heavy threads. For busy quilt tops, keep quilting motifs simple or use outlining. Outlining is a great techniques to emphasize patchwork blocks.

WAYS TO OUTLINE

When it comes to outlining blocks, you have several options: stitch in the ditch, curved outlining, or straight line contouring. Before you start stitching, it's helpful to map out the most efficient stitch path by doodling. Choose a lightweight thread in a color that blends with the fabric when using any of the techniques.

IN THE DITCH OUTLINING

Stitching in the ditch gives the shapes more definition. When possible, stitch on the inside of the block, in the "well" side of the seam allowances. You can stitch this free motion or machine guided (fig. A).

CURVED LINE OUTLINING

A quick free-motion way to outline pieced blocks is to stitch slightly curved lines from corner to corner within each shape of the block (fig. B). This method is faster and requires less precision than straight in-the-ditch outlining.

CONTOUR OUTLINING

Another way to outline a block is to connect alternate corners of the shape with chevron (V or inverted V) lines (fig. C). If the block is large enough, stitch multiple rows of chevrons to create a geometric design.

STITCHING PATH AND TRAVELING

When outlining pieced blocks, it's important to doodle to determine the most efficient stitching path. In some cases, the most efficient path requires that you overstitch a previous line of stitching. If you're using lightweight thread, the overstitched line may not be noticeable; however, if your thread is heavy, avoid overstitching to prevent an unwanted focal point. Try closely echo stitching the line instead or determine a different stitching path.

PRACTICE: TRIANGLES AND SQUARES BAR QUILT

In this practice session, you'll stitch in the ditch and outline shapes. Save your sample to complete in Lesson 25: Custom Quilting (page 122).

DOODLE

Squares, half-square triangles, and flying geese are three of the most common patchwork units found in quilts. In your sketchbook, draw three vertical columns, making the center column twice as wide as the left and right columns. Referring to the illustration on page 106, divide the left column into half-square-triangle units, the center column into flying-geese units, and the right column into squares. Try doodling all three methods of outlining in the columns.

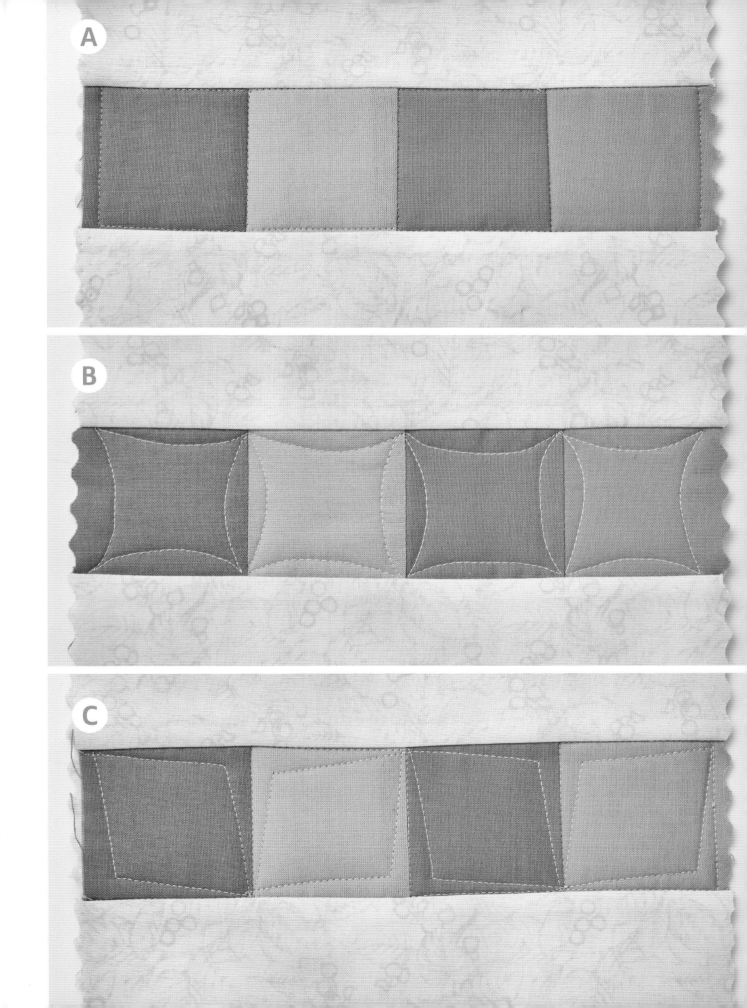

Use a vinyl overlay over a quilt block or a photo of a quilt block in a book or magazine. Again, try doodling all three methods of outlining. Determine the most efficient stitching path.

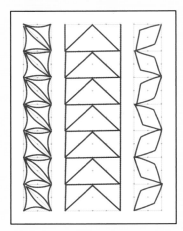

SUPPLIES

+ 1 quick quilt sandwich (page 14); see "Quilt Sandwich Option" below.

+ Top thread (heavyweight thread that contrasts well with the top fabric)

+ Bobbin thread (50-weight or lighter in a color that matches the top thread)

Quilt Sandwich Option

This lesson works best when stitching on a pieced quilt. Use a variety of prints and solids to make 22 half-square-triangle units measuring 2½" square, including seam allowances. Make 11 flying-geese units measuring 2½" × 4½", including seam allowances. Cut 22 squares, 2½" × 2½", and four strips, 2½" × 23". Referring to the photo on page 107, join the pieces to make a 20¼" × 23" sample. Layer and baste the quilt top, batting, and backing. If you want to get straight to quilting, see step 1 of "Get Ready," above right.

GET READY

1. If you aren't using a pieced quilt top, use white chalk and a ruler to mark the quilt top. Mark four vertical lines 2" apart on the left side. Repeat to mark four vertical line on the right side of the quilt sandwich. The center column should be 4" wide. Divide outer columns into 2" half-square-triangle units. On left side, skip a column and divide the next column into 2" squares. Repeat on the right side. Divide the center column into 2" × 4" flying-geese units.

2. Set up your machine for a machine-guided technique (see page 8).

STITCH

1. Stitch in the ditch on the marked vertical lines (or seamlines) to stabilize the quilt.

2. Switch your machine to a free-motion quilting setup. Stitch the shapes as follows.

+ Flying geese: stitch in the ditch

+ Squares: contour with chevrons

+ Half-square triangles: curved outlining

3. Set aside the quilt for Lesson 25: Custom Quilting (page 122).

EVALUATE

+ Which method, stitching in the ditch or outlining, looks the best?

+ Which method gives the pieced shapes the most definition?

+ Did you enjoy one style of outlining more than the other?

+ Did you doodle the stitching order before stitching?

+ Was the stitching order ever confusing?

+ Were you able to stitch most of the outlining without knotting off?

LESSON 22:

SPECIALTY THREAD

Fireflies that glow in the dark, stars that sparkle, and woolly mittens are all possible with the magic of specialty thread. Once you understand the qualities of basic threads and are comfortable with your machine's tension settings, it's fun to play with the magnificent variety of specialty threads.

USING SPECIALTY THREADS

Metallic, holographic, glow-in-the-dark, wool, monofilament, and many other thread types add beautiful special effects that can add drama to any quilt. However, specialty threads can be challenging for your machine to accommodate and may require special tools or techniques.

Slow down. When stitching with specialty threads it's often helpful to quilt slowly. If you're having trouble with the thread breaking, slow down. Not all threads can handle the stress of fast quilting as well as cotton thread can.

Adjust the tension. Most specialty threads require tension adjustment to create beautiful stitches and to prevent thread breakage. Test the tension settings before stitching with each type of specialty threads.

Use the right needle. A topstitch needle is great for stitching most specialty threads. It has a large eye and a deep groove to protect the thread as it travels into the bobbin area. Try a topstitch needle in the appropriate size to accommodate the thread.

Use a thread stand. Many specialty threads have memory and tend to coil as they travel off the spool. Remove the thread from the machine and use a thread stand or large mug instead to allow the thread more time to relax before it travels through the tension disks.

Try a thread lubricant. Thread lubricants, such as Sewer's Aid, can be very helpful in preventing thread breakage and skipped stitches. The lubricant can be applied along the spool of thread or to the needle using your fingertip. Always check your sewing-machine manual for recommendations.

Don't use special threads in the bobbin. Most specialty threads should not be placed in the bobbin. Stick with your favorite cotton or polyester thread in the bobbin.

PRACTICE: BUG JAR SAMPLER

In this practice session, you'll stitch a sampler using a variety of specialty threads.

SUPPLIES

+ 1 quick quilt sandwich (page 14)
+ Top thread (heavyweight thread that contrasts well with the top fabric)
+ Top threads (specialty threads such as NiteLite by Superior, Sulky Glowy, metallic threads, and monofilament for the bugs)
+ Bobbin thread (50-weight or lighter)
+ Heavy cardboard or cereal box
+ Lightweight paper
+ Glue stick

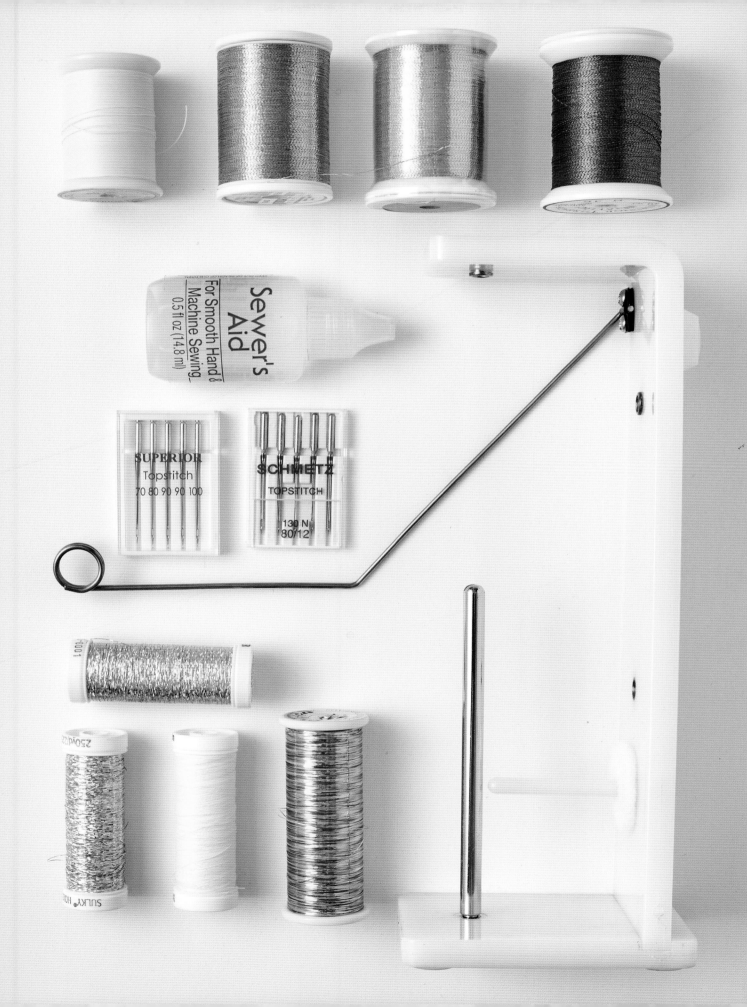

MAKE A TEMPLATE

Trace the bug jar pattern on page 11 onto lightweight paper. Roughly cut out the shape and glue it onto cardboard. Cut out the template directly on the line.

DOODLE

Trace the bug jar multiple times onto paper. Create a grid arrangement with the jars or design your own composition. Practice doodling bugs and butterflies or a simple flower motif in each jar.

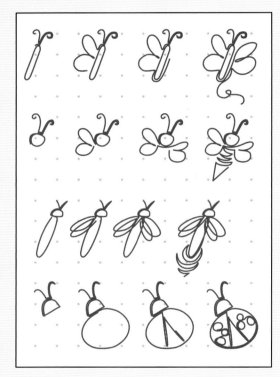

GET READY

1. Set up your machine for machine-guided quilting with a walking foot or even-feed mechanism (see page 8).

2. Use white chalk and a ruler to mark a 2 × 2 layout of 4" squares on the top fabric of the quilt sandwich. The squares should be 1" apart. Mark a 1"-wide border around the

perimeter of the squares. Trace around the jar template in the center of each 4" square.

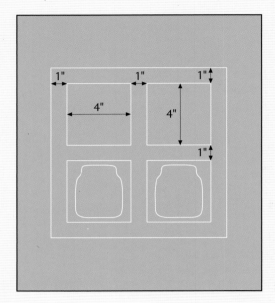

Make It Larger

If you'd like to sample many threads, make your grid larger and use your bug jar collection as a thread sampler.

STITCH

1. Using heavyweight thread, stitch the marked outlines of each of the boxes and the outer border line.

2. Set up your machine for free-motion quilting and outline the jars with the same thread or a new color. I stitched the squares with white thread, but used blue for my jars.

3. Choose a thread and stitch messy spirals and circles in the sashing areas. I used a blue-and-white variegated thread for the sashing.

4. Use a variety of threads to fill the jars with bugs or small flowers.

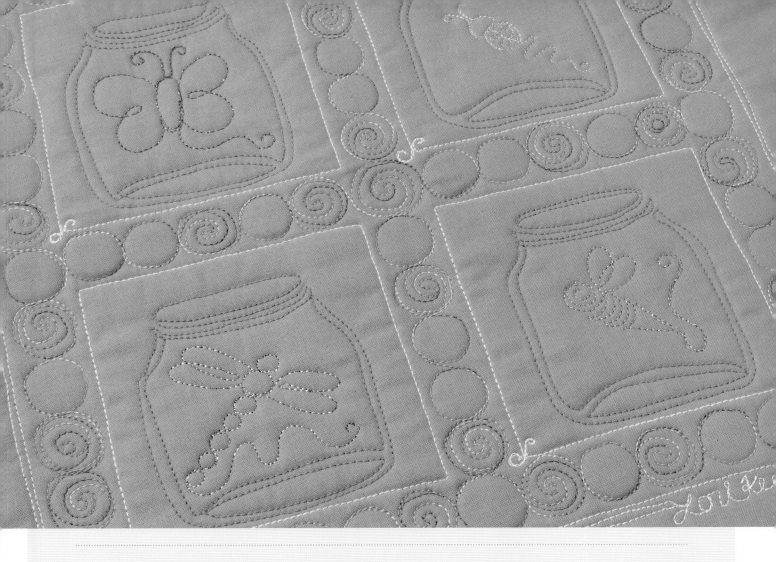

5. Echo stitch the outer line of the quilt and then complete the exercise by stitching your signature and the date..

6. Write the thread information on a piece of fabric and fuse it to the back of the quilt for the label.

EVALUATE

+ Do you have any specialty threads in your collection?

+ What motifs would benefit from being quilted with a special-effect thread?

+ What machine adjustments were required for each thread?

111

MACHINE QUILTING APPLIQUÉ BLOCKS

*When you take the extra time to appliqué quilt blocks, be sure
to show them off with quilting that enhances the shapes.*

QUILTING APPLIQUÉ BLOCKS

You can use several machine-quilting techniques to highlight and embellish appliqué. Avoid allover motifs that flatten rather than flatter the design elements.

DENSITY CONTRAST

Quilt sparsely within the appliqué and densely around the shape (fig. A). When stitched on high-loft batting, the effect is even more prominent. Grid motifs work well next to many appliqué shapes. Outline the appliqué with close echo stitching then stitch the grid or other background motifs around the shapes.

ECHO STITCHING

Echo stitching is a great way to turn appliqué motifs into focal points. Stitch around each appliqué, about ⅛" from the motif, to outline it. Then stitch one or more rows of echo stitching. Either fill an entire block with echo stitching or add a few rows of echo stitching and transition into a different motif (fig. B). By densely stitching around appliqué elements, the shapes are lifted above the surrounding area for more visual impact.

EMBELLISH WITH MOTIFS

After closely echo stitching the shape, add more detail to the appliqué using a quilting motif that enhances the appliqué. For example, add leaves around an appliqué flower (fig. C) or clouds around a sailboat appliqué.

NEGATIVE SPACE DESIGNS

Another way to add visual interest around appliqué is to repeat the appliqué shape as a negative space design. To create a negative space design, trace the appliqué shape near the appliquéd element and quilt around it densely. The unquilted, negative space will add visual interest to the nearby appliqué.

RAW-EDGE APPLIQUÉ

When machine quilting around raw-edge appliqué, it's helpful to stitch on and off the shape to help secure the edges and embellish the shape at the same time. Stitch several rows of wavy lines to blur the raw edges (fig. D).

ADD STITCHED DETAILS

If the appliqué is large, it may be necessary to stitch on top of the appliqué. Outline the shape and add stitched details to enhance the appliqué shape (fig. E).

PRACTICE: RAW-EDGE APPLIQUÉ

In this practice session, you'll stitch around appliquéd shapes.

DOODLE

For each appliqué, doodle a variety of quilting options. Plan how to travel from one motif to the next and choose a background motif. Use your vinyl overlay or a computer application like Procreate to test your design. Or go old school and doodle in your notebook!

SUPPLIES

+ 1 quilt sandwich with wool or high-loft polyester batting (page 14)

+ Fabric scraps for appliqué shapes

+ Fusible web

+ Top thread (choose threads for the background and to embellish the appliqués)

+ Bobbin thread (50-weight or lighter in a color that matches the top thread)

Appliqué Alternative

If you want to get straight to quilting, skip the appliqué and draw shapes on the quilt top using fabric markers. However, the results will have more impact if you do a bit of fusible appliqué.

1. *Apply fusible web to the wrong side of a variety of fabrics for appliqué.*

2. *Freehand cut several shapes to create a composition on your quilt sandwich.*

GET READY

1. Draw a large square or rectangle in the center of the quilt top.

2. Distribute the appliqués (or draw shapes) evenly over the quilt sandwich for an allover design, or cluster the motifs into a shape like a heart or wreath. Fuse the pieces in place with an iron following the fusible-web instructions.

3. Use chalk to mark a few more shapes to create negative space elements, such as the quilted leaves shown in fig. F.

4. Spool out several threads to audition them on your quilt.

5. Set up your machine for free-motion quilting.

STITCH

1. To compare the effects of echo quilting, echo stitch around some, but not all, of the elements.

2. To compare the effects of stitching on top of an appliqué, completely fill in one of the shapes with quilting.

114

3. For all other appliqué shapes, closely echo quilt around the first shape. Add rows of echo stitching and then travel to the next shape.

4. Stitch on and off the shape to blur the edge line. Stitch the shape two or three times then travel to the next shape. Continue to outline the shapes. Add echo stitching and motifs that embellish the appliqué.

5. Add a grid background to add density to the background and make the appliqué motifs stand out.

EVALUATE

✛ Compare an echo-stitched shape to one that was not echoed. Which is more prominent?

✛ Look at an appliqué with stitching on top; how does the quilting affect the look of the appliqué?

✛ Does the machine quilting enhance or detract from the appliqué design?

✛ Does the thread embellish and improve the design? If not, what would you change?

LESSON 24:

DESIGN TIPS

Machine quilting is much more than a way of holding the three layers of a quilt together. Use conventional design principles to create a balanced quilting design that enhances the quilt top. Because of the unique nature of quilting, I have some special tips to ensure good quilt design.

PLAN THE QUILT DESIGN

When choosing motifs and thread to highlight your quilt, it's helpful to remember a few design strategies.

PRINTS CONCEAL, SOLIDS REVEAL

Choose simple outlining techniques in areas of the quilt that are highly patterned either by complex piecing or printed fabrics. The quilted line is less visible in these areas (fig. A). On the other hand, stitch more complex or focal motifs on solid fabrics and areas of the quilt that have minimal piecing.

FOCAL POINT

To highlight an area or create a focal point, quilt the outline and surround it with dense quilting (fig. B). For example, to highlight appliqué, closely echo stitch around the shape, but add minimal details within the appliqué. When viewing the quilt, the most prominent focal points will be the areas with minimal quilting.

CONTRAST

Contrast is a design technique that draws your eye and adds interest to the quilted line. Contrast in machine quilting can be created in three ways: density, color, and shape contrast.

Density contrast occurs where a sparsely quilted area is positioned next to a heavily quilted area (fig. C). The heavily quilted area recedes and the lightly quilted area becomes a focal point. Motifs like Grid Pop (fig. D) takes advantage of density contrast.

Color contrast is achieved by choosing thread that's a different color or value than the fabric. Motifs stitched in contrasting color will be more visible than threads stitched with matching thread. Choose contrasting thread to create focal motifs and use matching thread to create texture motifs (figs. D and F).

Shape contrast aids in creating focal points within the quilted line. Stitch straight-line motifs next to curvy motifs to make both motifs more visible (fig. E).

REPEAT AND VARY

Choose a few motifs and repeat them in several areas of the quilt to create a cohesive quilt design (fig. F). Vary the motifs in scale or stitch partial patterns to accommodate the various shapes within the blocks, borders, and sashing. Repeat shapes and patterns from the quilt top in the quilting designs to reinforce the quilt's design. For example, repeat appliqué shapes in the machine-quilting motifs.

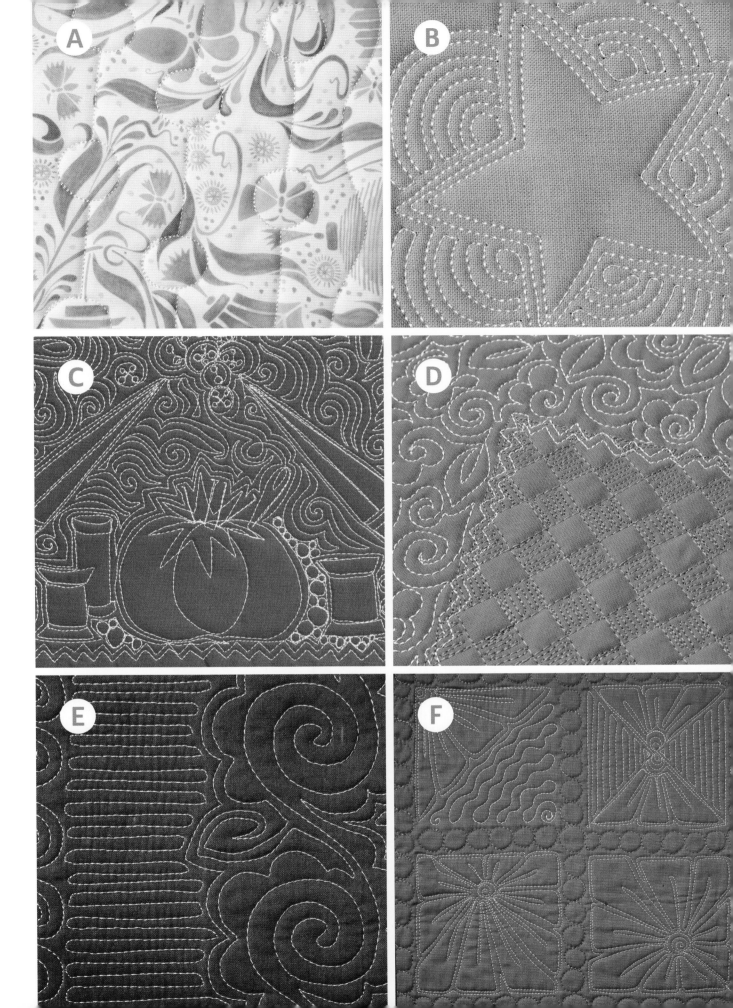

STYLE

The quilted line adds an important dimension to the overall style of the quilt. Geometric patterns add a modern touch to a quilt while feathers and flowers may be more traditional (fig. G). Be sure to choose motifs that advance the quilt style, but don't be afraid to mix styles.

PERSONALITY AND THEME

Choose motifs that reflect the theme of the quilt or reflect an interest of the recipient. Add butterflies and bees to a floral quilt or stitch stars and stripes on a patriotic quilt. If the recipient likes to cook, stitch pies and cupcakes. Guitars (fig. H) are perfect for the music lover in your life!

BALANCE

To create a balanced composition and to keep the quilt from distorting, space the amount of stitching evenly over the quilt. It's okay to have areas with dense stitching and lighter stitching, but these differences should be evenly distributed throughout the quilt.

SCALE

When quilting on a sewing machine, the larger the quilt, the smaller the motifs will need to be. It's difficult to move the weight and bulk of a large quilt quickly and freely enough to create long smooth lines. Consequently, quilts stitched on sewing machines tend to have denser quilting than quilts completed on a long-arm machine.

Once you've chosen a motif, doodle the pattern in different sizes to determine the best scale for your quilt design. Some motifs can be scaled larger or smaller without changing any of the lines. For example, you can stitch a circle with a ¼" or 4" diameter. Other motifs look better when the motif is altered slightly. To make a motif smaller, you may want to leave out details, whereas when making a motif larger, it may be better to add echo stitching or other details.

Consider whether you'll be able to move the quilt easily enough to create the motif. Small motifs require precise control and large motifs require moving the bulk of the quilt smoothly.

PRACTICE: POLKA DOT TABLE RUNNER

In this practice session, you'll stitch a table runner, creating contrast solely through the quilting.

DOODLE

Doodle Twist, circles, and semicircles. Doodle Twist with very little spacing to create a dense fill pattern around the circles and semicircles.

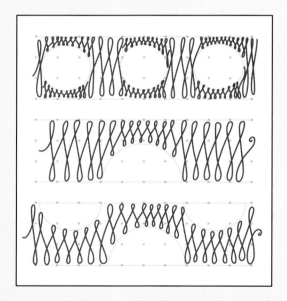

SUPPLIES

+ 1 quilt sandwich, 18" × 40", with medium-weight cotton or polyester batting (page 14)

+ Top thread (lightweight thread that matches the top fabric, heavyweight thread that matches the top fabric, and heavyweight thread that contrasts well with the top fabric)

+ Bobbin thread (50-weight or lighter in a color that matches the top thread)

+ Cup or mug

118

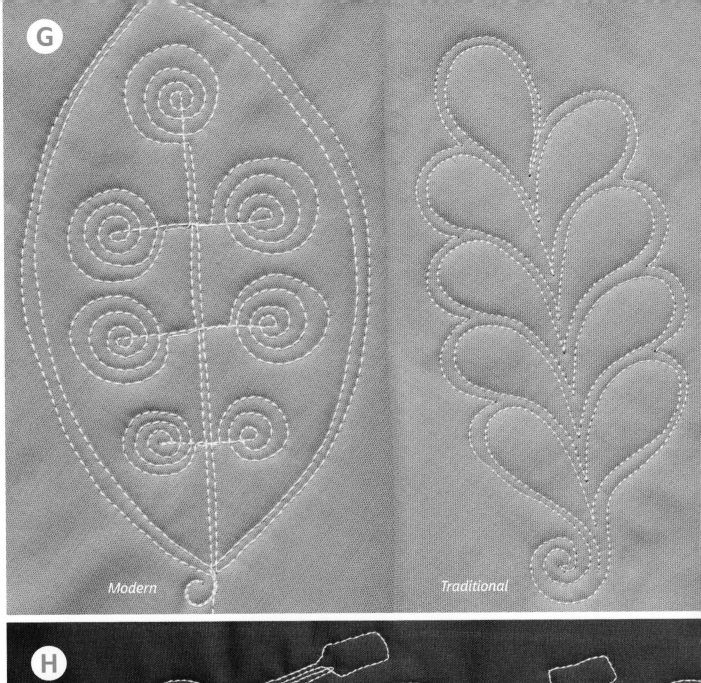

Modern   Traditional

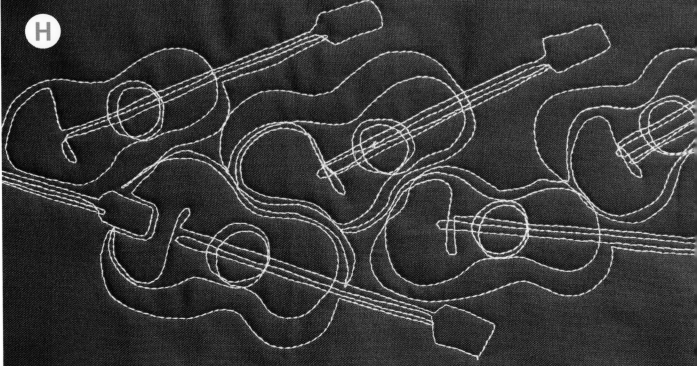

GET READY

1. Mark vertical and horizontal center lines on the quilt sandwich to use as reference. On each short end, draw a line 5" from the outer edge. On each long side, draw a line 6" from the outer edge. Then draw a line 1½" inside each previous marked line.

2. On each short end, trace around a cup or mug to mark semicircles between the top and bottom marked lines and outer edges.

3. On both sides, use a ruler to mark lines 1½" apart in the 6"-wide borders.

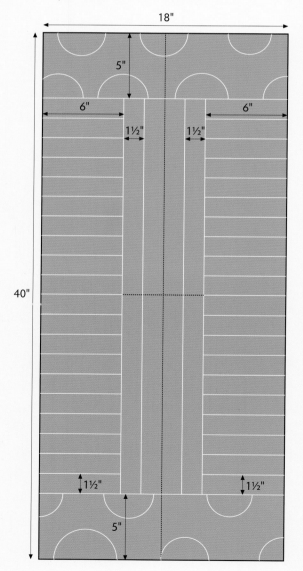

4. Set up your machine for machine-guided quilting (page 8).

STITCH

1. Stitch the marked border lines using lightweight thread. Do not stitch the short parallel lines in the side borders.

2. Switch your machine to a free-motion quilting setup. Using heavyweight thread that matches the top fabric, stitch Twist in the 1½"-wide columns.

3. Switch to a different color of heavyweight thread to complete the rest of the quilt, and stitch as follows:

+ Stitch spirals in the center column.

+ Quilt the outlines of the semicircles, stitching off the quilt or on top of the previous line of stitching to travel between motifs.

+ Stitch the Twist motif between the semicircles.

+ Stitch the Dots and Dashes motif along the marked lines in the 6"-wide borders. Travel off the quilt where possible and on the center marked line to complete the motif in one pass.

4. Complete the exercise by stitching your signature and the date.

EVALUATE

+ What is your favorite motif?

+ Could you use the basic framework of this table runner and fill it with two of your favorite motifs?

+ Could you complete a quilt in your collection with a few simple motifs?

LESSON 25:

CUSTOM QUILTING

Custom quilting combines a variety of techniques and materials to elevate a quilt top from a one-dimensional project to a three dimensional work of art. This seems like a tall order, but custom quilting can be accomplished with a few simple techniques and a step-by-step design plan.

CREATE A PLAN

The first thing to do when creating a custom quilt is to create a design plan. A design plan should include the type of batting, motifs, and thread. It's not necessary to have the entire plan created before beginning to stitch. Sometimes it's easiest to start stitching sections where the plan is clear and add to the design plan as you progress.

EVALUATE THE ENTIRE QUILT

Look at the quilt as a whole and consider the overall theme and style of the quilt. Take a picture or draw a sketch of the entire quilt. Or hang the quilt top where you can refer to it frequently. Think about the style and theme of the quilt as well as who it's for and how it will be used. Use this information to choose the batting type, thread for stabilizing, and motifs for each section.

Batting. Choose a batting that will enhance the style of the quilt. Consider all the sections of the quilt and any special effects you're trying to achieve.

Thread for stabilizing. Use a lightweight thread in a color that blends with most of the fabrics.

Motifs by section. Look at the sections of the quilt, such as the border, sashing, blocks, or group of blocks that are similar. Each section will require a separate design plan. Take photos or draw a sketch of each section. Include the dimensions and other notes about the section. In your doodle notebook, draw the shapes you would like to fill with machine quilting.

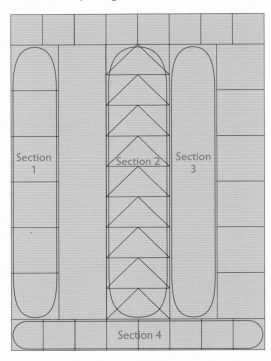

CHOOSE MOTIFS

For each section, choose two or three motifs with good contrast that fit the style and theme of your quilt. Whenever possible, look for quilt motifs that repeat shapes or motifs found in the quilt top. For example, if the quilt top is embellished with circles, consider motifs like Dots and Dashes (page 50).

AUDITION MOTIFS

Audition the motifs you've selected by doodling. Use a vinyl overlay or computer application to test the motif in the shape and size found in the quilt. Sometimes, a thumbnail sketch looks great, but when the motif is stretched to a larger size, the design falls flat. Modify the scale as shown above, or try partial designs to highlight your quilt top.

CHOOSE THREAD

Select thread for one section of the quilt at a time. Consider your design goals. Do you want the quilting to be focal point, texture, or both? Choose thread accordingly. You may need one or more thread for each section of the quilt.

DESIGN AND STITCH

Work through the design process for each section of the quilt. Choose motifs and thread and start stitching one section at a time, even if you haven't planned every section. It can be enlightening to work on your quilt while designing. The act of quilting helps you to see and feel how the thread, batting, and motifs are working together and you can make design decisions as you stitch.

PRACTICE: CUSTOM QUILTING

In this practice session, we'll finish the sample started in Lesson 21: Outlining Basic Shapes (page 104).

QUILT DESIGN

Look at the quilt as a whole and consider theme, style, and how it will be used. You've already chosen and completed basting and stabilizing the quilt. It's time to divide the quilt into sections for design. This quilt has four sections: flying geese, half-square triangles, squares, and solid vertical bars. We've already completed the design plan and stitched the first three sections. Now it's time to create a design plan for the final section—the solid bars.

DOODLE

In your sketchbook, draw a thumbnail of the quilt and a few vertical columns. Doodle motifs to fill the solid bars. Choose one motif and audition it on the quilt using the vinyl overlay. Try several options and choose your favorite.

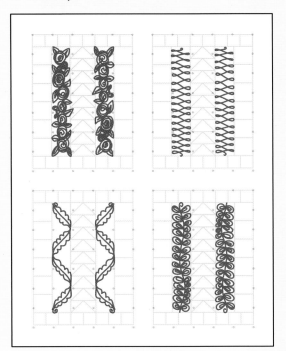

SUPPLIES

+ Quilt sandwich from Lesson 21: Outlining Basic Shapes

+ Top thread (heavyweight thread that contrasts well with the top fabric or lightweight thread to create a textured design)

+ Bobbin thread (50-weight or lighter in a color that matches the top thread)

GET READY

1. Mark the quilt if necessary.

2. Set up your machine for quilting (see page 8).

STITCH

Stitch your favorite design in the vertical bars of the quilt. Complete all the stitching in one section before moving on to a new section.

EVALUATE

+ Overall, how did your quilt turn out?

+ Which section is your favorite?

+ Which was the most fun to quilt?

+ Is there a section of a quilt top in your collection that you're ready to design and quilt?

WRAP UP—YOU'RE ON YOUR WAY

Congratulations! You've committed to becoming a better machine quilter and through 25 lessons, you've done it! You've doodled and stitched and studied and compared. You've created nearly 21 projects and sampled a wide variety of thread, batting, motifs, compositions, and techniques.

YOUR OWN DESIGN STYLE

You can now look forward to free-motion quilting with confidence, knowing that you can embellish and personalize your quilts with style. You now have the knowledge to choose the right materials to create quilts that reflect your design style and know how to adjust your machine to create beautiful stitches. You've doodled and stitched many hours to improve the fluency of your stitches, and you've developed a repertoire of motifs you can use in many ways.

The goal of the lessons in this book was for you to sample as many machine-quilting materials, supplies, and techniques as possible. From this sampling, you can choose the techniques and materials that work best for you. To streamline your work flow, choose your favorite methods and materials as your "go-to" way to create a design or complete a quilt top.

PRACTICE: TAKE STOCK

Gather all your lesson samples and review each one. Compare the first project with the latest. Are you more comfortable? Have your stitches improved? Are you more adventurous about choosing threads and motifs?

CONTINUE ON YOUR JOURNEY

Machine quilting is like any skill; you get better the more you practice! Develop your style by editing out the parts you don't enjoy and focusing on your favorite techniques, designs, and materials.

+ **Doodle every day.** Doodling improves stitch fluency and sparks creativity. It's an important part of the machine-quilting process.

+ **Learn new motifs.** Motifs are the mainstay of machine quilting. Challenge yourself to learn a new motif every week and combine motifs to create quilts with personality.

+ **Try new supplies.** Once you have your "go-to" supplies, try new threads, battings, and fabric to create different effects. New products often inspire new design ideas!

+ **Make and use samples.** Samples are the cure for disappointment in quilting and they can be fun to make! Create samples to try out new materials, techniques, and motifs before you use them on your quilts. Turn your samples into completed mini-quilts or pillows.

+ **Review your quilt-top collection.** Pick a quilt top and batting, baste the quilt, and start stabilizing. While you're stabilizing, doodle and plan the next section of the quilt.

+ **Most of all, have fun!** If you have fun while you're quilting, your quilts will be fun and fun quilts become well-loved heirlooms! We'd LOVE to see what YOU create! Please share your quilts! #LoriKennedyQuilts #MartingaleTPP

ABOUT THE AUTHOR

Lori Kennedy is an incurable doodler and quilting fanatic who loves to help quilters add fun and personality to their quilts with whimsical designs. Lori is a Bluprint instructor and a Bernina Ambassador. She writes the My Line column in *American Quilter* magazine and can be found on her blog, LoriKennedyQuilts.com, offering "Tuesday Tutorials" and daily inspiration.